- Fuerteventura Travel Guide 2025: *Uncove*

Fuerteventura
Travel Guide 2025:

Uncover the Island's Secrets

David O. Terry

David O. Terry

Copyright © David O. Terry 2024

This book may not be reproduced, stored in a retrieval system or transmitted in any form or means, electronic, mechanical, photocopying, recording, or otherwise, without the prior permission of the copyright owner.

Design concept by
Cornerstone Details Resource Ltd.

• **Fuerteventura Travel Guide 2025:** *Uncover the Island's Secrets* •

Table of Contents

My Visit to Fuerteventura 7

Introduction 12

    Welcome to Fuerteventura 12

    How to Use This Guide 13

    A Brief History of Fuerteventura 17

Getting There and Around 21

    Flights and Transportation Options 21

    Navigating the Island: Car Rentals, Public Transport, and Taxis 24

    Important Travel Tips and Essentials 28

    Conclusion 31

Top Attractions in Fuerteventura 32

    Corralejo Natural Park 32

    Jandía Peninsula 34

    Betancuria: Fuerteventura's Historic Heart 36

    Ajuy Caves and Coastal Walks 38

    Oasis Park Fuerteventura 40

    Conclusion 42

Hidden Gems of Fuerteventura 43

    Off-the-Beaten-Path Beaches 43

    Untouched Villages and Towns 46

    Secret Viewpoints and Hikes 48

    Local Markets and Artisan Crafts 50

Conclusion 51

Beaches and Watersports in Fuerteventura 53
Best Beaches for Sunbathing 53

Surfing, Windsurfing, and Kitesurfing Hotspots 56

Diving and Snorkeling Locations 58

Family-Friendly Beaches and Activities 60

Conclusion 63

Outdoor Adventures in Fuerteventura 64
Hiking Trails and Nature Walks 64

Cycling Routes Across the Island 67

Exploring Volcanoes and Lava Fields 69

Wildlife Watching and Birding 71

Conclusion 72

Cultural Experiences in Fuerteventura 74
Traditional Festivals and Events 74

Local Cuisine and Dining Guide 77

Museums and Cultural Centers 80

Art, Music, and Performances 82

Conclusion 84

Where to Stay in Fuerteventura 85
Best Resorts and Hotels 85

Budget-Friendly Accommodations 88

Unique Stays: Eco-Lodges, Boutique Hotels, and More 90

Camping and Glamping on the Island 92

Conclusion 94

Dining and Nightlife in Fuerteventura 95

Top Restaurants for Authentic Cuisine 95

Street Food and Local Delicacies 98

Bars, Clubs, and Nightlife Spots 100

Wine Tasting and Local Breweries 103

Conclusion 104

Shopping and Souvenirs in Fuerteventura 106

Best Places to Shop 106

Local Crafts and Artisanal Products 109

Fuerteventura Markets: What to Buy 113

Conclusion 115

Practical Information for Visiting Fuerteventura 117

Health and Safety Tips 117

Language and Local Customs 120

Money, Banking, and Tipping 121

Emergency Contacts and Services 123

Conclusion 125

Day Trips and Excursions in Fuerteventura 126

Island Hopping: Exploring the Canary Islands 126

Guided Tours and Activities 129

Road Trips and Scenic Drives 132

Conclusion 135

Sustainability and Responsible Travel in Fuerteventura 136

Eco-Friendly Travel Tips 136
Supporting Local Communities 139
Conservation and Wildlife Protection 142
Conclusion 145

Conclusion 146

• **Fuerteventura Travel Guide 2025:** *Uncover the Island's Secrets* •

My Visit to Fuerteventura

From the moment my plane began its descent into Fuerteventura, I knew I was about to experience something extraordinary. The island unfolded beneath me like a vast, golden canvas dotted with volcanic peaks, shimmering beaches, and patches of green that stood out against the arid landscape. I had read about Fuerteventura's windswept beauty, but seeing it with my own eyes gave me an immediate sense of awe and excitement. I had traveled to this island, one of the jewels of the Canary Islands, in search of something different—an escape from the familiar, a break from the everyday routine. Little did I know that Fuerteventura would offer me much more than just a holiday—it would become an adventure that would leave a lasting imprint on my heart.

As I stepped off the plane and felt the warm breeze brush my skin, the island's energy hit me right away. It wasn't just the warmth of the sun or the dry, earthy smell of the land that struck me—it was a feeling of freedom. It was as though time itself had slowed down, urging me to take a deep breath and let go of everything I'd left behind. The airport in **Puerto del Rosario** was small and unassuming, a perfect gateway to an island that didn't try too hard to impress. Fuerteventura wasn't about grandeur or excess; it was about simplicity, raw beauty, and an invitation to connect with nature and the local culture.

I picked up my rental car, a small, sturdy SUV perfect for exploring the island's rugged roads, and set off toward **Corralejo**, my first destination. The drive was breathtaking from the very start. To my right, the shimmering Atlantic Ocean stretched out endlessly, while to my left, the land revealed its volcanic past through jagged peaks and black lava fields. The wind, a constant companion on this island, swirled through my open windows as I cruised along the coast. It felt like Fuerteventura itself was whispering to me, calling me to explore its hidden corners.

My first stop was **Corralejo Natural Park**, home to the island's iconic sand dunes. As I pulled into the parking area, I was greeted by an endless expanse of creamy, rolling dunes that seemed to go on forever. I kicked off my shoes and stepped onto the warm sand, feeling it shift beneath my feet. The dunes stretched out toward the sea, creating a stunning contrast between the soft sand and the brilliant blue of the Atlantic. I climbed the nearest dune and stood at the top, gazing out over the surreal landscape. The view took my breath away. To the west, the volcanic peaks of **Montaña Roja** loomed in the distance, while to the east, the ocean sparkled under the midday sun.

I spent the next hour wandering through the dunes, letting my mind drift as the wind played with my hair. There was something deeply calming about the solitude of this place. The only sounds were the faint rustle of the wind and the occasional cry of a seabird soaring overhead. I felt like I was in another world—far from the chaos and noise of everyday life. It was the perfect introduction to Fuerteventura, and I knew I had only scratched the surface of what this island had to offer.

• **Fuerteventura Travel Guide 2025:** *Uncover the Island's Secrets* •

Later that afternoon, I made my way into **Corralejo** town. The vibe was completely different from the tranquility of the dunes. Corralejo was alive with the hum of people enjoying their holiday, the clinking of glasses in beachfront cafes, and the laughter of children playing in the shallow waters of the beach. I found a little seafood restaurant by the harbor called **La Vaca Azul**, known for its fresh, locally caught fish. I ordered **pulpo a la gallega**, a dish of tender octopus drizzled with olive oil and sprinkled with paprika, along with a cold glass of Canarian white wine. As I sat there, savoring the flavors and watching the boats bob in the marina, I felt an incredible sense of peace. This was what I had come for—to slow down, to experience life at a different pace.

The next day, I decided to venture south, making the long but scenic drive to the **Jandía Peninsula**. The landscape shifted as I drove—the volcanic terrain giving way to rolling hills and open plains. The road twisted and turned through rugged mountains before finally revealing the stunning coastline of **Playa de Sotavento**. I had heard stories about this beach, a favorite among windsurfers and kitesurfers, and as I approached, I could see the colorful kites dotting the sky, dancing in the wind. The beach was vast, with shallow lagoons forming at low tide, creating natural pools of turquoise water.

I spent the afternoon wandering along the shore, the soft sand beneath my feet and the wind whipping around me. At one point, I found myself completely alone, with nothing but the sound of the waves and the wind. It was a moment of pure tranquility—a feeling of being completely immersed in nature. The wild beauty of Fuerteventura had cast its spell on me, and I found myself falling more and more in love with the island with every passing moment.

One of the most memorable experiences of my trip came when I visited **Cofete Beach**. I had read that the journey to Cofete was not for the faint of heart—a bumpy dirt road winding through the mountains of the Jandía Peninsula—but I was determined to see this legendary beach for myself. As I navigated the narrow, winding road, the landscape became more and more dramatic. Jagged cliffs rose up on either side, and the road hugged the edge of the mountain, offering heart-stopping views of the ocean far below.

When I finally arrived at Cofete, the view was even more breathtaking than I had imagined. The beach stretched out for miles, completely wild and untouched, with the imposing **Jandía Mountains** rising steeply behind it. There was a sense of isolation here, as if I had reached the end of the world. I walked along the shore, the wind howling around me, the waves crashing against the sand. It was one of the most awe-inspiring places I had ever been. The sheer scale of the landscape made me feel small, in the best possible way.

As the days passed, I continued to explore the island, each day bringing new discoveries. I hiked through volcanic craters, watched dolphins play in the waters off **Morro Jable**, and visited the charming village of **Betancuria**, where time seemed to stand still. I wandered through local markets, picking up handmade pottery and tasting the island's famous **Queso Majorero**. I even ventured to an aloe vera farm in **Lajares**, where I learned about the plant's healing properties and bought natural skincare products made right there on the farm.

Fuerteventura was everything I had hoped for and more. It was a place where I could disconnect from the noise and reconnect with myself, a place where nature and simplicity were celebrated. As I prepared to leave the island, I felt a twinge of sadness. Fuerteventura had given me something invaluable—a sense of freedom, of peace, of adventure. I knew that this island, with its wind-swept beauty and gentle rhythm, would always hold a special place in my heart.

And as my plane lifted off from **Puerto del Rosario**, I glanced out the window at the golden sands and blue waters below, already planning my return to this magical place.

Introduction

Welcome to Fuerteventura

Welcome to **Fuerteventura**, a place where time seems to slow down, and the only pressing decision is whether to lounge on its golden beaches or explore its rugged volcanic landscapes. As the second-largest island in the Canary Islands, Fuerteventura often feels like a well-kept secret, offering its visitors a perfect mix of relaxation, adventure, and cultural experiences.

Known for its striking contrasts, Fuerteventura greets you with dramatic landscapes that span from vast, rolling sand dunes to craggy volcanic hills and idyllic beaches with turquoise waters that seem to stretch endlessly into the horizon. The island, located just 100 kilometers off the coast of North Africa, is blessed with more than 3,000 hours of sunshine annually, making it a year-round destination for sunseekers. But Fuerteventura's appeal goes beyond its picture-perfect shores. It's a place where the wind and the waves dance in harmony, creating a paradise for water sports enthusiasts, while its untouched interior offers those seeking tranquility a peaceful retreat into nature.

Fuerteventura may not have the bustling nightlife or urban appeal of its sister islands, such as Tenerife or Gran Canaria, but that's part of its charm. Life on this island moves at its own pace. The days are long, leisurely affairs spent savoring fresh seafood, walking through whitewashed villages, or perhaps hiking up one of its volcanic peaks to watch the sun dip below the horizon. It's the perfect destination for anyone looking to escape the stresses of modern life and reconnect with nature, history, and the simple pleasures of life.

Whether you're drawn to Fuerteventura for its world-class kitesurfing and windsurfing spots, its dramatic landscapes, or simply the desire to relax in a place where nature feels raw and unspoiled, you'll find that this island has something special for every type of traveler. Its windswept beauty is captivating, and once you've dipped your toes in its waters and felt the island's energy, you might just find it hard to leave.

In this guide, you'll discover the hidden gems, stunning attractions, and local tips that will help you make the most of your time on Fuerteventura. Whether it's your first visit or you're returning to rediscover the island, we hope this guide will enrich your journey and inspire you to explore all that Fuerteventura has to offer.

Welcome to Fuerteventura, your adventure awaits.

How to Use This Guide

This guide has been thoughtfully crafted to help you experience Fuerteventura to the fullest, whether you're here for a short weekend escape, a two-week holiday, or a longer stay. From practical advice on how to get around to in-depth suggestions on the best beaches, restaurants, and hidden gems, this guide will be your trusted companion throughout your stay.

Here's how to get the most out of it:

1. **Planning Your Arrival and Getting Around**

   Before you even set foot on the island, we'll make sure your journey is smooth. The chapter on transportation offers detailed insights on how to get to Fuerteventura, whether by plane or ferry, and the best ways to navigate the island once you're here. We'll cover rental car options, public transportation routes, cycling opportunities, and even walking trails for those who prefer a slower pace.

2. **Exploring Fuerteventura's Top Attractions**

   In the attractions section, you'll find a curated list of must-see sights—from iconic beaches like *Corralejo Natural Park* to the historic town of *Betancuria*. But beyond the tourist hotspots, we'll guide you to less-crowded areas where you can soak in the island's natural beauty at your own pace. Whether you're an adventurer looking to scale a volcano or someone who prefers to sip wine by the beach, this chapter will give you plenty of ideas for filling your days.

3. **Finding the Best Beaches**

   The beaches of Fuerteventura are what dreams are made of—whether it's the endless sands of *Sotavento* or the quiet, tucked-away coves near *El Cotillo*. This guide will help you choose the right beach for your mood. Want to surf? We've got you covered. Prefer a secluded, naturist-friendly beach to escape the crowds? No problem. From family-friendly beaches to adrenaline-pumping surf spots, there's a beach for every occasion.

4. **Experiencing the Local Culture and Cuisine**

   A trip to Fuerteventura wouldn't be complete without diving into the local culture, and food is a big part of that. In this guide, you'll find suggestions for everything from trying the island's famous **Queso Majorero** (a goat cheese with a distinct flavor) to sipping local wines or indulging in fresh seafood. We'll also take you through the island's traditional festivals, markets, and local customs so you can truly connect with Fuerteventura's culture.

5. **Getting Active**

   For adventure seekers, the island offers endless opportunities. Fuerteventura is known as a haven for windsurfing and kitesurfing, and you'll find all the tips you need to try these thrilling sports—even if you're a complete beginner. If you prefer land-based activities, we'll also introduce you to the island's hiking and cycling trails, wildlife reserves, and more.

6. **Where to Stay**

   This guide includes a detailed section on where to stay, based on your travel style and preferences. From luxury beachfront resorts to cozy, eco-friendly lodges and budget-friendly apartments, we've covered all bases.

We'll help you choose the best base for your stay, whether you want to be in the heart of the action or tucked away in a peaceful village.

7. **Practical Information**

   Our practical information chapter will cover everything you need to know to have a stress-free visit. From tips on local customs and language to health and safety advice, money matters, and emergency contacts, you'll have all the essential details at your fingertips.

8. **Suggested Itineraries**

   If you're overwhelmed by all the possibilities or simply want a tried-and-tested plan to follow, don't worry. We've provided sample itineraries tailored to different types of travelers—from families with young kids to solo adventurers. These itineraries are designed to help you experience the very best of Fuerteventura in the time you have.

Feel free to dive into the sections that interest you the most. This guide is designed to be flexible, so whether you're a planner or a spontaneous traveler, you can use it however best suits your style.

A Brief History of Fuerteventura

Ancient Origins and Indigenous Settlers

Fuerteventura's history begins long before European settlers arrived on its shores. Like the other islands in the Canary Archipelago, Fuerteventura was born out of volcanic activity millions of years ago, its landscapes shaped by both fire and wind. But the first known human inhabitants, believed to have arrived between 1000 and 200 BCE, were the **Majos** or **Guanche** people, descendants of Berber-speaking North African tribes.

These early settlers brought with them a simple but effective way of life. Living in small villages, they practiced subsistence farming, fished the abundant waters around the island, and raised goats—an animal still central to Fuerteventura's identity today. While they lived modestly, these indigenous people had a rich culture, as evidenced by the archaeological remains found across the island, including tools, pottery, and cave paintings.

The Majos were also skilled navigators, but their relative isolation meant they were cut off from the greater Mediterranean and European worlds for centuries, leading to a unique, self-sufficient way of life. Their influence can still be felt today in the island's culture, particularly in the persistence of goat herding, traditional crafts, and ancient place names.

The European Conquest and the Birth of Betancuria

The peace and solitude of the island would be forever altered in 1402 when **Jean de Béthencourt**, a Norman nobleman under the Spanish crown, landed on Fuerteventura during his conquest of the Canary Islands. Unlike on some of the other islands, the indigenous people offered relatively little resistance to the European conquerors, and Béthencourt soon established the first European settlement at **Betancuria**, which became the island's capital.

Béthencourt's arrival marked the beginning of significant changes on the island. The European settlers brought new crops, livestock, and, most importantly, the Christian faith. The Majos, who had no immunity to European diseases and were unaccustomed to their new rulers' ways, saw their population decline sharply in the years that followed. Gradually, the local population was absorbed into the colonial system.

Betancuria grew into a small but important administrative and religious center. The **Santa María Church**, built shortly after Béthencourt's arrival, became the heart of the island's Christian community. Despite its remote location, the town played a key role in the island's early economy, thanks to its fertile valleys where crops could be grown.

Pirates, Poverty, and Resilience

During the 16th and 17th centuries, Fuerteventura was often subject to pirate attacks. Its remote location and lack of fortifications made it an easy target for pirates seeking to plunder the island's meager resources. These attacks devastated many communities, and the island's isolation meant that it had little external support.

The people of Fuerteventura, however, were resilient. Life on the island was hard, with its arid climate making large-scale farming difficult. Yet, the inhabitants made the most of their land, relying heavily on goat farming, fishing, and small-scale agriculture to survive. The island's famous **Queso Majorero** (goat cheese) became an important product, providing not only sustenance but also a valuable commodity for trade with other islands.

Modern Fuerteventura: From Isolation to Tourism

Fuerteventura's fortunes began to change in the mid-20th century, as advances in air travel and tourism brought new opportunities to the island. The opening of the airport in 1969 marked the beginning of Fuerteventura's transformation from a sleepy, agrarian island to a thriving tourist destination.

The island's natural beauty, with its endless beaches, dramatic landscapes, and year-round sunshine, quickly attracted visitors from across Europe and beyond. By the 1980s, Fuerteventura had established itself as a popular destination for sunseekers, particularly among those looking for a quieter alternative to the more developed Canary Islands.

Today, Fuerteventura is a thriving island that balances its tourism industry with a deep respect for its cultural heritage and natural environment. Efforts to promote sustainable tourism have helped preserve much of the island's unspoiled landscapes, while traditional industries like goat farming and artisanal crafts continue to thrive alongside modern resorts and restaurants.

The island may have changed dramatically since the days of the Majos and European settlers, but Fuerteventura's spirit of resilience and adaptability remains. Visitors today will find an island that is both steeped in history and alive with the energy of the present—where ancient traditions coexist with modern comforts, and nature reigns supreme.

Whether you're interested in exploring the island's historic sites, hiking through its volcanic landscapes, or simply enjoying its tranquil beaches, Fuerteventura's history adds a rich layer of depth to any visit. The island's story is one of survival, adaptation, and quiet strength—a story that continues to unfold as Fuerteventura welcomes the world while holding on to its unique identity.

Fuerteventura Travel Guide 2025: *Uncover the Island's Secrets*

Getting There and Around

Fuerteventura is one of those rare destinations where getting there feels like the beginning of an adventure, and traveling around the island offers endless opportunities to explore at your own pace. As the second-largest of the Canary Islands, Fuerteventura boasts a variety of landscapes and experiences, from remote beaches to bustling towns. Whether you're flying in from afar or hopping over from a neighboring island, getting to Fuerteventura is straightforward. Once on the island, you'll find plenty of transportation options to suit your travel style, whether you prefer the freedom of renting a car, exploring by bus, or using taxis.

In this chapter, we'll cover the ins and outs of arriving in Fuerteventura, navigating the island once you're here, and offer some essential travel tips to ensure your journey is smooth and enjoyable.

Flights and Transportation Options

Getting to Fuerteventura by Air

Fuerteventura is well connected to major European cities and is served by **Fuerteventura Airport (FUE)**, also known as *El Matorral Airport*. The airport is located about 5 kilometers (3 miles) south of the capital, **Puerto del Rosario**, and serves as the main gateway to the island for international and domestic travelers alike. Whether you're flying in from mainland Spain, another Canary Island, or a European hub, getting to Fuerteventura by air is usually the most convenient option.

- **International Flights**: Fuerteventura Airport receives a large number of direct flights from across Europe, particularly during the high tourist season (October to April). If you're flying in from major cities such as London, Berlin, Paris, Madrid, or Amsterdam, you'll likely find direct flights operated by both low-cost carriers and traditional airlines. Airlines such as Ryanair, easyJet, Jet2, Iberia, Vueling, and TUI fly frequently to the island, making it accessible for travelers on a range of budgets. During the winter months, Fuerteventura becomes especially popular among those escaping colder climates, and additional seasonal flights are added to meet the demand. Flights from the UK and Germany are particularly frequent.
- **Domestic Flights**: If you're already in Spain or visiting another Canary Island, you'll find several domestic flight options. **Binter Canarias** and **Vueling** offer regular flights between Fuerteventura and the other Canary Islands (Gran Canaria, Tenerife, Lanzarote, La Palma, etc.), as well as flights to mainland cities like Madrid, Barcelona, and Seville. These flights are usually short—between 40 minutes to an hour—and can be a great way to island-hop or extend your Spanish adventure.
- **Airport Facilities**: Fuerteventura Airport is small but modern, offering a range of services for arriving and departing travelers. You'll find car rental desks, a few cafes, shops (including a duty-free shop), ATMs, and free Wi-Fi throughout the airport. Given its size, the

airport is easy to navigate, and you won't face the long lines or crowded terminals typical of larger airports.

Arriving by Ferry

If you prefer a slower, more scenic journey to Fuerteventura, or if you're already in the Canary Islands, taking a ferry is a popular option. Several ferry services connect Fuerteventura with neighboring islands, particularly **Lanzarote** and **Gran Canaria**.

- **From Lanzarote**: The ferry between **Playa Blanca** in Lanzarote and **Corralejo** in Fuerteventura is one of the most frequent and shortest routes, with the crossing taking only about 30 to 45 minutes. Ferries are operated by **Fred Olsen Express**, **Naviera Armas**, and **Líneas Romero**, and run multiple times per day. This makes it an ideal option if you're spending time in Lanzarote and want to hop over to Fuerteventura for a few days or vice versa.
- **From Gran Canaria**: For a longer journey, you can take a ferry from **Las Palmas** in Gran Canaria to **Morro Jable** in Fuerteventura. The trip takes around 2 to 3 hours, depending on the service, and is operated by **Fred Olsen Express** and **Naviera Armas**. This ferry route offers scenic ocean views and a relaxed way to travel between two of the largest Canary Islands.
- **From Tenerife**: While less common, there are ferry services between **Santa Cruz de Tenerife** and **Morro Jable** or **Puerto del Rosario**. The journey is significantly longer, often taking 6 to 8 hours, so it's

more suitable for travelers with plenty of time who want to enjoy the scenic voyage between islands.

Ferries typically have onboard amenities such as restaurants, bars, and seating areas, with some offering upgraded seating or cabins for longer journeys. It's advisable to book your ferry tickets in advance, especially during peak travel periods or holidays.

Navigating the Island: Car Rentals, Public Transport, and Taxis

Once you've arrived in Fuerteventura, getting around the island is relatively easy. Whether you want the flexibility of your own vehicle, the convenience of public transport, or the occasional taxi ride, there are multiple ways to explore.

Car Rentals: The Ultimate Freedom

For most travelers, renting a car is the best way to explore Fuerteventura. The island's vast landscapes and remote beaches are often best accessed by car, and having your own set of wheels allows you to move at your own pace. Whether you're staying in one of the island's main towns or plan to venture off the beaten path, renting a car provides the freedom to discover the island's hidden gems.

- **Rental Companies**: Major international car rental companies like **Avis**, **Hertz**, **Europcar**, and **Sixt** all operate in Fuerteventura, along with several local companies such as **Cicar** and **TopCar**. You'll find rental desks at the airport, as well as in major towns like Corralejo, Caleta de Fuste, and Morro Jable. It's a good idea to book your rental car in advance, especially during peak tourist season when demand is higher.

- **Driving in Fuerteventura**: Driving on the island is generally straightforward, with well-maintained roads connecting the major towns, resorts, and attractions. The main roads, such as the **FV-1** (which runs along the east coast between Corralejo and Puerto del Rosario) and the **FV-2** (which runs from Puerto del Rosario down to the southern tip in Morro Jable), are in excellent condition. Some rural roads leading to more remote beaches or hiking trails may be unpaved, but they are usually passable with a standard vehicle.
- **Parking**: Parking is generally easy to find across the island. Most towns offer free parking, though you might find paid parking areas in busy tourist spots like Corralejo or Caleta de Fuste. In rural areas, you can usually park on the roadside near beaches or trailheads.
- **Costs**: Car rental prices vary depending on the season, type of car, and rental duration. On average, expect to pay between **€25 and €50 per day** for a standard car. Fuel prices in Fuerteventura are generally lower than on mainland Europe, and gas stations are easily found throughout the island.

Public Transport: The Budget-Friendly Option

If you prefer not to drive, Fuerteventura has a reliable and affordable public transport system, though it may not be as convenient if you want to explore more remote areas.

- **Buses**: The island's bus network is operated by **Tiadhe**, and it connects most towns and tourist destinations. The buses are modern, air-conditioned, and comfortable, making them a great option for budget-conscious travelers. Some key bus routes include:
    - **Line 3**: Puerto del Rosario – Caleta de Fuste – Las Salinas
    - **Line 6**: Corralejo – Puerto del Rosario
    - **Line 10**: Puerto del Rosario – Morro Jable

Bus fares range from **€1.50 to €10**, depending on the distance traveled, and tickets can be purchased directly from the driver. There's also the option of purchasing a **Bono Bus** card, which offers discounted fares and can be recharged.

The downside of relying on buses is that schedules can be less frequent, particularly in the more remote parts of the island. If you plan to visit more isolated beaches or attractions, you may need to combine public transport with taxis or walking.

Taxis: Convenient and Plentiful

Taxis are widely available across the island, and they offer a convenient way to get around, particularly for short distances or when public transport isn't available.

- **Taxi Availability**: You'll find taxi ranks in all major towns, at the airport, and outside popular tourist spots. Taxis in Fuerteventura are easily recognizable by their white color and green taxi lights. You can also hail a taxi on the street or book one by phone.
- **Fares**: Taxi fares are regulated, and the meter starts at around **€3.00**, with additional charges depending on distance traveled. Short trips within towns usually cost around **€5 to €10**, while longer journeys between towns can range from **€20 to €50**. Keep in mind that fares increase slightly during nighttime hours and on public holidays.
- **Tips for Using Taxis**: Most taxi drivers in Fuerteventura speak some English, especially in tourist areas, but it's always a good idea to have your destination written down. Tipping is not required, but rounding up the fare or adding a small tip is appreciated.

Cycling and Walking

For those who enjoy a more active way of exploring, **cycling** is a great option, particularly in the flatter parts of the island. There are several scenic cycling routes, particularly along the coast. Fuerteventura's roads are generally cyclist-friendly, and many of the smaller towns have bike rental shops offering

mountain bikes, **electric bikes**, and **standard bicycles** for daily or weekly hire.

- **Popular Cycling Routes**: The coastal route from **Corralejo to El Cotillo** is a favorite for cyclists, offering stunning ocean views along the way. You can also cycle through the interior of the island, particularly around **Betancuria**, where the landscapes are more rugged and less trafficked.

If you enjoy walking, **Fuerteventura** also offers plenty of opportunities for hikers and walkers, with trails crisscrossing the island. Many of the island's smaller towns and villages are also easily explored on foot, making walking a great way to immerse yourself in the local culture.

Important Travel Tips and Essentials

Weather and Packing

Fuerteventura enjoys a **subtropical climate**, with warm temperatures year-round. However, the island can be quite windy, particularly on the northern and eastern coasts, so it's important to pack accordingly.

- **Clothing**: Light, breathable clothing is ideal for most of the year, but it's a good idea to bring a light jacket or sweater for cooler evenings, especially if you're visiting during the winter months. Don't forget your swimwear, as Fuerteventura's beaches are one of its main attractions.

If you plan to hike, bring sturdy walking shoes, sunscreen, and a hat to protect yourself from the sun.
- **Sun Protection**: The Canary Islands are located close to the equator, so the sun can be intense even on cooler days. Bring plenty of sunscreen with a high SPF and reapply it frequently, especially if you're spending time on the beach or in the water.

Money Matters

- **Currency**: The official currency in Fuerteventura is the **Euro (€)**. Credit and debit cards are widely accepted in most hotels, restaurants, and shops, but it's always a good idea to carry some cash, especially if you plan to visit smaller towns or markets.
- **ATMs**: ATMs are easily found in most towns and tourist areas, so withdrawing cash is usually not a problem. However, be mindful of potential foreign transaction fees if using a card from outside the Eurozone.

Language and Communication

- **Language**: The official language in Fuerteventura is **Spanish**, but English is widely spoken in tourist areas. In more remote parts of the island, you may encounter fewer English speakers, so learning a few basic Spanish phrases can be helpful.
- **Wi-Fi and Internet**: Most hotels, cafes, and restaurants offer free Wi-Fi, so staying connected shouldn't be an issue. However, if you plan to explore rural or remote areas, internet access may be limited.

Health and Safety

- **Health Care**: Fuerteventura has a good standard of health care, with several hospitals and medical centers across the island. For minor illnesses or injuries, pharmacies (*farmacias*) are widely available and can provide over-the-counter medications.
- **Travel Insurance**: It's recommended to have travel insurance that covers medical expenses, particularly if you plan to participate in adventure sports like windsurfing or hiking. European Union citizens can also use their **European Health Insurance Card (EHIC)** for medical treatment.

Tipping

- **Tipping**: Tipping is not mandatory in Fuerteventura, but it's customary to leave a small tip for good service. In restaurants, rounding up the bill or leaving a **5-10% tip** is appreciated. For taxi drivers, rounding up the fare is common.

Respecting the Environment

Fuerteventura's natural beauty is one of its biggest draws, and efforts are being made to preserve its landscapes. As a visitor, it's important to respect the island's environment by minimizing waste, recycling, and not disturbing wildlife. When hiking or visiting natural areas, always stick to marked trails and avoid leaving litter behind.

Conclusion

Getting to and around Fuerteventura is part of the adventure. Whether you choose the freedom of a rental car, the convenience of public transport, or the simplicity of a taxi ride, exploring the island at your own pace is one of the best ways to uncover its hidden beauty. With its stunning beaches, charming villages, and breathtaking landscapes, Fuerteventura invites you to slow down, enjoy the journey, and discover the wonders that await at every turn.

• *David O. Terry* •

Top Attractions in Fuerteventura

Fuerteventura's beauty lies in its stunning natural landscapes, charming towns, and rich cultural heritage. As the second-largest Canary Island, it offers a wide variety of attractions that cater to all types of travelers—from nature lovers and history buffs to adventure seekers and families. Whether you're here to bask on its pristine beaches, explore its volcanic landscapes, or immerse yourself in the island's history, Fuerteventura has something to offer at every turn.

This chapter will take you through some of the island's must-see attractions, each of which reveals a different side of Fuerteventura's diverse character. From the rolling sand dunes of Corralejo to the ancient volcanic caves of Ajuy, these top spots will leave you spellbound and eager to explore more.

Corralejo Natural Park

A Landscape Like No Other

Located in the northeast of Fuerteventura, **Corralejo Natural Park** (*Parque Natural de Corralejo*) is one of the island's most iconic attractions and a paradise for nature enthusiasts. Covering over 2,600 hectares, the park is home to some of the most dramatic landscapes in the Canary Islands, with vast stretches of golden sand dunes, rugged volcanic terrain, and pristine beaches.

- **The Sand Dunes**: One of the park's most famous features is its **immense sand dunes**, which seem to stretch endlessly towards the horizon. These dunes are made from fine, white sand that has been blown inland from the Atlantic Ocean over thousands of years. Walking through this landscape feels almost like being in the Sahara Desert—except that you can spot the sparkling blue waters of the Atlantic in the distance.

The dunes are a popular spot for photography, hiking, and even sandboarding, but they're also a place to simply relax and soak in the surreal beauty of the surroundings. The best time to visit is in the early morning or late afternoon when the light is soft, and the shadows cast by the dunes create stunning patterns across the sand.

- **Beaches**: The beaches within Corralejo Natural Park are some of the finest on the island, offering soft sand and crystal-clear waters. **Playa del Moro**, **Playa del Viejo**, and **Playa de los Martos** are perfect for swimming, sunbathing, and water sports like windsurfing and kitesurfing. The beaches are typically less crowded than those near the town of Corralejo, giving you plenty of space to stretch out and enjoy the sun.
- **Volcanic Landscapes**: In addition to the dunes, the park is home to striking volcanic landscapes, particularly the **Montaña Roja** (Red Mountain), an extinct volcano that rises above the flat expanse of sand. A short hike to the summit offers panoramic views of the park, the nearby island of **Lobos**, and the town of Corralejo. The contrast between the black volcanic rock and the white sand is truly breathtaking.

- **How to Get There**: Corralejo Natural Park is located just south of the town of Corralejo, making it easily accessible by car, bike, or even on foot. If you're driving, you can park along the **FV-1 road**, which runs parallel to the park. There are no facilities within the park itself, so be sure to bring water, snacks, and sun protection.

Visiting Corralejo Natural Park is a must for anyone traveling to Fuerteventura. Whether you're a photographer looking for the perfect shot or simply want to lose yourself in the natural beauty, the park's dunes and beaches will leave a lasting impression.

Jandía Peninsula

Wild, Rugged, and Unspoiled

In the southern part of Fuerteventura lies the **Jandía Peninsula**, a region of stunning contrasts, where vast, untouched beaches meet dramatic mountains and hidden valleys. The peninsula is home to some of the island's most beautiful and remote landscapes, offering a sense of wild, unspoiled beauty that's hard to find elsewhere.

- **Cofete Beach**: One of the main highlights of the Jandía Peninsula is **Cofete Beach**, often considered one of the most beautiful and remote beaches in the Canary Islands. This 12-kilometer stretch of golden sand is framed by the imposing **Jandía Mountains** on one side and the crashing waves of the Atlantic on the other. Despite its beauty, Cofete remains largely untouched by development, making it a true escape from the hustle and bustle of modern life.

Getting to Cofete is part of the adventure. The beach is accessed by a rough dirt road that winds through the mountains, offering stunning views along the way. While a 4x4 vehicle is recommended for the journey, those who make the trip are rewarded with a pristine beach where they can often have the sand all to themselves. Swimming here can be dangerous due to strong currents, but the experience of walking along this wild, untamed shoreline is unforgettable.

- **Pico de la Zarza**: For hikers, the **Pico de la Zarza** is a must-visit. As the highest point on Fuerteventura, standing at 807 meters (2,648 feet), the hike to the summit offers breathtaking views of the entire peninsula, including the beaches of Cofete and **Playa de Sotavento**. The trail is well-marked and takes about 3 to 4 hours to complete, depending on your pace. Along the way, you'll pass through rugged volcanic terrain, with the occasional sighting of local wildlife, such as Barbary squirrels and ravens.
- **Playa de Sotavento**: On the eastern side of the peninsula, **Playa de Sotavento** offers a completely different beach experience. Known for its turquoise waters and shallow tidal lagoons, Sotavento is a paradise for water sports enthusiasts, particularly kitesurfers and windsurfers. The beach is also a great place for sunbathing and swimming,

with long stretches of soft sand and plenty of space to spread out.

If you're not into water sports, the sheer beauty of Sotavento's coastline is reason enough to visit. The sandbanks and lagoons that form at low tide create a constantly shifting landscape, making every visit feel like a new discovery.

- **How to Get There**: The Jandía Peninsula is located at the southern tip of Fuerteventura, about 90 kilometers from Puerto del Rosario. Most visitors base themselves in the resort town of **Morro Jable**, which offers a range of accommodation and dining options. From Morro Jable, you can easily reach the beaches and hiking trails by car or join one of the many guided tours that explore the peninsula.

The Jandía Peninsula is the perfect destination for travelers looking to experience Fuerteventura's wild side. Whether you're hiking through its mountains, relaxing on its beaches, or kitesurfing in its lagoons, the sense of isolation and untouched beauty is what makes this region so special.

Betancuria: Fuerteventura's Historic Heart

A Step Back in Time

Tucked away in a lush valley in the center of the island, **Betancuria** is Fuerteventura's historic heart and one of the most picturesque towns in the Canary Islands. Founded in 1404 by the French explorer **Jean de Béthencourt**, Betancuria was the island's first capital and served as its political and religious center for centuries. Today, the town retains much of its colonial charm, with whitewashed buildings, cobblestone streets, and a peaceful, laid-back atmosphere.

- **Santa María Church**: One of the main attractions in Betancuria is the **Iglesia de Santa María**, a beautiful church that dates back to the 15th century. Although the church was partially destroyed by pirates in the 16th century, it was later rebuilt and remains one of the finest examples of Canarian architecture on the island. Inside, you'll find stunning woodwork, religious artifacts, and a peaceful courtyard that's perfect for quiet reflection.
- **Betancuria Museum**: For those interested in the island's history, the **Museo Arqueológico de Betancuria** offers a fascinating glimpse into Fuerteventura's past. The museum houses a collection of artifacts from the island's pre-Hispanic period, including pottery, tools, and statues left behind by the indigenous **Majo** people. It's a small but informative museum that provides valuable insight into the island's early inhabitants and the challenges they faced.
- **Streets and Squares**: Betancuria is best explored on foot, and wandering through its narrow streets and quiet squares feels like stepping back in time. The town's colonial architecture, with its whitewashed walls and red-tiled roofs, is beautifully preserved, and there are several charming cafes and shops where you can enjoy a coffee or pick up a souvenir.

- **Surrounding Nature**: Betancuria is located within the **Betancuria Rural Park**, a protected area that offers some of the island's most stunning landscapes. The park is crisscrossed with hiking trails that take you through volcanic mountains, lush valleys, and scenic viewpoints. The **Mirador de Morro Velosa**, located just outside the town, offers panoramic views of the island's interior and is a great spot to watch the sunset.
- **How to Get There**: Betancuria is located about 30 kilometers west of Puerto del Rosario and can be reached by car via the **FV-30** road. The drive to Betancuria is scenic, with winding roads that offer stunning views of the surrounding countryside. There are also buses that run to the town from Puerto del Rosario, though they are infrequent, so renting a car is the best option if you want to explore at your own pace.

Betancuria is a must-visit for anyone interested in Fuerteventura's history and culture. Its tranquil atmosphere, historic buildings, and beautiful surroundings make it a perfect destination for a day trip or a relaxing stop on your island adventure.

Ajuy Caves and Coastal Walks

A Window into Fuerteventura's Geological Past

Located on the island's rugged west coast, the **Ajuy Caves** (*Cuevas de Ajuy*) offer a fascinating glimpse into Fuerteventura's geological history. These ancient sea caves, some of which date back more than 70 million years, are among the oldest geological formations in the Canary Islands. In addition to the caves, the nearby village of **Ajuy** is a charming fishing community with a black sand beach and stunning coastal walks.

- **Exploring the Caves**: The Ajuy Caves are a series of large sea caves that were formed by volcanic activity and erosion over millions of years. As you explore the caves, you'll see layers of volcanic rock that tell the story of Fuerteventura's turbulent geological past. The largest cave is particularly impressive, with a wide entrance and high ceilings that allow you to walk deep into the rock.

    The path to the caves begins at **Playa de Ajuy**, a black sand beach that contrasts beautifully with the turquoise waters of the Atlantic. From the beach, a well-marked trail leads along the cliffs to the caves, offering stunning views of the coastline along the way. It's a relatively easy walk, but be sure to wear sturdy shoes, as the path can be rocky in places.

- **Coastal Walks**: In addition to the caves, the area around Ajuy is perfect for coastal walks. The **Ajuy to Puertito de los Molinos** trail takes you along the dramatic cliffs of the west coast, passing through rugged landscapes and offering panoramic views of the Atlantic. The walk is about 5 kilometers each way and is a great way to experience the wild beauty of Fuerteventura's less-visited western shores.

- **The Village of Ajuy**: The village of Ajuy is a small but charming fishing community where time seems to have

stood still. After exploring the caves and cliffs, you can relax at one of the village's seafood restaurants, where fresh fish and local dishes are served with views of the ocean. The black sand beach is also a peaceful spot to unwind, though the waves here can be strong, so swimming is not always advisable.
- **How to Get There**: Ajuy is located about 50 kilometers west of Puerto del Rosario and can be reached by car via the **FV-30** and **FV-621** roads. There is a small parking area near the beach, and the village is easily explored on foot.

Visiting the Ajuy Caves is like stepping into a prehistoric world, where the island's ancient geological forces are on full display. Combined with the charm of the village and the beauty of the surrounding coast, it's a must-see destination for nature lovers and history enthusiasts alike.

Oasis Park Fuerteventura

A Family-Friendly Adventure in Nature

For a change of pace from the beaches and mountains, **Oasis Park Fuerteventura** offers a fun and educational day out for families and animal lovers. Located in the south of the island, near the village of **La Lajita**, this large wildlife park and botanical garden is home to over 3,000 animals, as well as a variety of exotic plants. It's one of the largest animal parks in the Canary Islands and provides a great opportunity to get up close and personal with wildlife from around the world.

- **Animal Encounters**: One of the highlights of Oasis Park is the chance to interact with the animals. You can feed giraffes, walk through an aviary filled with colorful birds, and even take a camel ride through the park. The park is home to a wide variety of species, including elephants, hippos, zebras, meerkats, and reptiles, and there are several animal shows and demonstrations throughout the day.

  The **sea lion show** and the **bird of prey demonstration** are particularly popular with visitors, offering a chance to learn more about these incredible animals while seeing them in action.

- **Botanical Garden**: In addition to the wildlife, Oasis Park is home to a beautiful **botanical garden** that showcases a wide variety of plants from around the world. The garden is particularly well known for its collection of cacti and succulents, with thousands of species on display. It's a peaceful place to wander and enjoy the beauty of the natural world, and there are plenty of shaded areas where you can relax and take a break from the sun.

- **Conservation and Education**: Oasis Park is dedicated to conservation and education, and the park participates in several international breeding programs for endangered species. Visitors can learn about the park's efforts to protect wildlife and preserve natural habitats through interactive exhibits and guided tours.

- **Dining and Facilities**: The park offers several dining options, including a restaurant that serves traditional Canarian cuisine and a café with snacks and refreshments. There are also picnic areas, a playground for children, and a gift shop where you can pick up souvenirs.
- **How to Get There**: Oasis Park is located about 10 kilometers from the resort town of **Costa Calma** and is easily accessible by car or bus. The park offers a free shuttle service from several major tourist areas, including **Morro Jable** and **Caleta de Fuste**.

Oasis Park Fuerteventura is a fantastic day out for families, animal lovers, and anyone looking to learn more about the natural world. With its wide variety of animals, interactive experiences, and beautiful gardens, it's a place where both kids and adults can enjoy a memorable adventure.

Conclusion

Fuerteventura's top attractions offer something for everyone, whether you're drawn to its natural beauty, historic sites, or wildlife. From the vast dunes of Corralejo to the wild beaches of the Jandía Peninsula, the island's diverse landscapes will leave you in awe. Betancuria's rich history and the geological wonders of the Ajuy Caves provide a deeper connection to Fuerteventura's past, while Oasis Park offers a fun and educational experience for families. No matter what kind of traveler you are, these top attractions are sure to make your visit to Fuerteventura unforgettable.

Hidden Gems of Fuerteventura

While Fuerteventura's top attractions often steal the spotlight, there's a quieter, more intimate side to the island that awaits those willing to venture off the beaten path. Beyond the popular beaches and well-known tourist spots lies a wealth of hidden gems—places that capture the true essence of Fuerteventura, where the pace is slower, the landscapes more untouched, and the experiences feel personal. These are the corners of the island that many visitors miss, but those who take the time to explore them are rewarded with unspoiled beauty, authentic local culture, and a deeper connection to the island's soul.

In this chapter, we'll guide you to some of Fuerteventura's lesser-known treasures, from secluded beaches and quiet villages to secret hiking trails and local markets where you can experience the island's rich artisan traditions. Whether you're looking for solitude, adventure, or a glimpse into the island's rural life, these hidden gems will give you a new perspective on Fuerteventura.

Off-the-Beaten-Path Beaches

Fuerteventura is famous for its beaches, but not all of them are packed with sunbeds and tourists. If you're looking for a more tranquil experience, the island is dotted with secluded coves and untouched stretches of sand that offer peace and solitude.

- **Playa de Esquinzo** (Northwest)

Located on Fuerteventura's northwest coast, near the village of **El Cotillo, Playa de Esquinzo** is a quiet, wild beach that feels a world away from the bustling resorts. With its soft golden sand, clear waters, and dramatic cliffs, Esquinzo is a perfect spot for those seeking solitude and natural beauty. The beach is often uncrowded, even during peak season, and its remote location means you're more likely to share the sand with a few surfers or local families than with hordes of tourists.

The waves at Esquinzo can be strong, making it popular among surfers, but it's also a great place for a long, peaceful walk along the shore. The surrounding cliffs offer some protection from the wind, and there are a few sheltered spots where you can set up for the day. There are no facilities here, so make sure to bring your own food, water, and sun protection. Esquinzo's rugged beauty and quiet atmosphere make it one of Fuerteventura's best-kept secrets.

- **Playa de Jarugo** (West Coast)

If you're willing to travel a bit further off the beaten path, **Playa de Jarugo** is one of the most remote and unspoiled beaches on the island. Tucked away on Fuerteventura's wild west coast, this hidden gem is only accessible by a dirt track, but the journey is well worth it. When you arrive, you'll find a small, crescent-shaped bay framed by dramatic cliffs and volcanic rock formations.

The beach's black volcanic sand contrasts beautifully with the turquoise waters, creating a striking visual experience. Due to its isolated location, Playa de Jarugo is often completely deserted, offering the perfect escape for those looking to unwind in nature. The waves here can be powerful, so it's not ideal for swimming, but the sense of peace and seclusion is unmatched.

As with many of the island's lesser-known beaches, there are no facilities at Jarugo, so be sure to pack everything you'll need for the day. The beach is best accessed by car, and the dirt road can be rough, so a four-wheel-drive vehicle is recommended.

- **Playa de Garcey** (West Coast)

For beachgoers with an adventurous spirit, **Playa de Garcey** offers not only a beautiful stretch of sand but also a bit of history. Located on the west coast of the island, Playa de Garcey was once the final resting place of the **SS American Star**, a shipwreck that became a local landmark. While the wreck has largely disappeared into the sea in recent years, the beach itself remains a peaceful, isolated spot where the crashing waves and dramatic cliffs set the scene for a memorable visit.

The beach is relatively quiet, with few visitors, and its remote location means you'll often have the sand to yourself. The ocean here is rough, so it's not the best beach for swimming, but it's a fantastic spot for photography, beachcombing, or simply soaking in the raw beauty of the coastline. The road to Garcey is unpaved, so it's best to visit with a 4x4 vehicle.

Untouched Villages and Towns

While Fuerteventura's coastal towns tend to attract the most visitors, the island's interior and less-visited areas are home to charming villages that have preserved their traditional way of life. These towns offer a glimpse into the island's rural past, where time seems to move more slowly, and the rhythms of life are dictated by the seasons.

- **Pájara**
  Nestled in the foothills of the **Betancuria Massif**, the village of **Pájara** is one of Fuerteventura's most picturesque and peaceful spots. Its whitewashed buildings, cobbled streets, and leafy squares create a serene atmosphere that invites visitors to slow down and enjoy the simple pleasures of village life. Pájara is perhaps best known for its beautiful church, the **Iglesia de Nuestra Señora de Regla**, which features an intricately carved stone façade with Aztec-inspired motifs—a unique detail that sets it apart from other churches on the island.

The village is surrounded by green fields and palm trees, a rare sight in Fuerteventura's arid landscape, and it makes for a lovely place to wander or enjoy a meal in one of its quiet restaurants. Don't miss the chance to try some local Canarian dishes, such as **papas arrugadas** (wrinkled potatoes) or fresh goat cheese, at a traditional village eatery.

- **Tiscamanita**

  For a taste of Fuerteventura's agricultural heritage, the village of **Tiscamanita** offers a quiet retreat into the heart of the island's rural traditions. Located in the central plains of Fuerteventura, Tiscamanita is known for its **windmills**, which were once used to grind **gofio**, a traditional Canarian flour made from roasted grains. You can visit the **Centro de Interpretación de los Molinos**, a small museum that offers insight into the island's agricultural history and the importance of windmills in the local economy.

  The village itself is small and sleepy, with narrow streets lined with whitewashed houses and bougainvillea-draped walls. It's a great place to stop for a quiet stroll, chat with the friendly locals, or enjoy a coffee in the village square.

- **Ajuy**

  Although known for its **caves** and **black sand beach**, the village of **Ajuy** on Fuerteventura's west coast is also a hidden gem worth exploring. This tiny fishing village has managed to retain its old-world charm, and visiting it feels like stepping back in time. The small harbor is home to colorful fishing boats that bob in the water, while the village's simple houses and narrow streets offer a glimpse into traditional Canarian life.

Ajuy's restaurants serve up some of the freshest seafood on the island, and you'll often see fishermen unloading their catch of the day as you enjoy your meal. The village's laid-back vibe, combined with its rugged coastal beauty, makes it a perfect spot for a leisurely afternoon away from the busier tourist areas.

Secret Viewpoints and Hikes

Fuerteventura's landscapes are best appreciated from above, and the island is home to several secret viewpoints and hiking trails that offer spectacular vistas and a sense of adventure. Whether you're looking for a challenging trek through volcanic terrain or a peaceful walk with panoramic views, these hidden spots are sure to reward your efforts.

- **Pico de la Zarza** (Jandía Peninsula)

    If you're up for a challenge, the hike to the summit of **Pico de la Zarza** is one of the most rewarding in Fuerteventura. As the island's highest point, standing at 807 meters, Pico de la Zarza offers unparalleled views of the **Jandía Peninsula** and the beaches of **Cofete** and **Sotavento**. The trail is well-marked, but it's a steep climb that takes about 3 to 4 hours to reach the top.

Once at the summit, you'll be greeted with panoramic views that stretch out over the Atlantic Ocean, with the rugged, volcanic landscape of Fuerteventura below you. It's a place where you can truly appreciate the island's raw beauty and vast, unspoiled wilderness.

- **Mirador de Morro Velosa**

Located near Betancuria, the **Mirador de Morro Velosa** is a lesser-known viewpoint that offers sweeping views of Fuerteventura's interior. Designed by the famous Canarian artist **César Manrique**, the mirador blends seamlessly into the surrounding landscape, with its natural stone structure offering a peaceful place to sit and take in the views.

From the lookout, you can see the rolling hills, valleys, and volcanic peaks that make up Fuerteventura's rural heartland. The view is especially stunning at sunset, when the light casts a golden glow over the island. There's also a small exhibition inside the building that provides information about the geology and history of Fuerteventura.

- **Barranco de los Encantados** (The Enchanted Ravine)

For a more off-the-beaten-path hiking experience, head to the **Barranco de los Encantados**, also known as the **Barranco de los Enamorados** (The Lovers' Ravine). This hidden gem is located near the village of **La Oliva** and is famous for its otherworldly rock formations, which have been shaped by wind and water over thousands of years.

The hike through the ravine takes you past surreal, sculpted sandstone formations that resemble natural sculptures. It's a peaceful and relatively easy walk, making it a great option for those who want to explore Fuerteventura's unique geology without too much strenuous effort. The ravine is rarely crowded, so you'll often have the trail to yourself, allowing you to fully immerse yourself in the natural beauty.

Local Markets and Artisan Crafts

Fuerteventura's rich artisan traditions are alive and well, and the island is home to several local markets where you can discover handmade goods, fresh produce, and traditional crafts. These markets offer a chance to connect with local artisans, farmers, and makers, and to take home a piece of Fuerteventura's culture with you.

- **Mercado de los Tradiciones (La Oliva)**

    Held every Tuesday and Friday morning in the town of **La Oliva**, the **Mercado de los Tradiciones** is a great place to discover local products and handmade crafts. The market features stalls selling everything from fresh fruits and vegetables to handmade pottery, jewelry, and leather goods. It's a vibrant, bustling place where you can chat with local artisans, sample some traditional foods, and pick up unique souvenirs to take home.

Fuerteventura Travel Guide 2025: *Uncover the Island's Secrets*

- **Mercado Agrícola de Puerto del Rosario**

  For a more authentic taste of Fuerteventura's agricultural heritage, head to the **Mercado Agrícola** in **Puerto del Rosario**. Held every Saturday morning, this farmers' market offers a wide range of local produce, including fresh fruits, vegetables, cheeses, and baked goods. It's a great place to buy ingredients for a picnic or to stock up on local delicacies like **Queso Majorero**, a delicious goat cheese that's one of Fuerteventura's most famous products.

- **Feria Insular de Artesanía (Antigua)**

  If you happen to be visiting Fuerteventura in May, don't miss the **Feria Insular de Artesanía** in **Antigua**. This annual craft fair is one of the largest artisan markets in the Canary Islands and attracts craftspeople from across the archipelago. Here, you'll find a wide variety of traditional Canarian crafts, including handwoven textiles, pottery, wooden carvings, and more. It's a fantastic opportunity to see local artisans at work and to take home a truly unique piece of Fuerteventura's cultural heritage.

Conclusion

Fuerteventura's hidden gems offer a quieter, more intimate side of the island that's often missed by the typical tourist. Whether you're wandering through untouched villages, relaxing on a secluded beach, or hiking to a secret viewpoint, these lesser-known spots allow you to connect with the island in a deeper, more personal way. By stepping off the beaten path, you'll discover a Fuerteventura that's rich in natural beauty, cultural traditions, and unforgettable experiences—one that will stay with you long after you've left its shores.

Beaches and Watersports in Fuerteventura

Fuerteventura is often described as a beach lover's paradise—and with good reason. Its coastline is dotted with some of the most beautiful and diverse beaches in the Canary Islands. From vast stretches of golden sand to intimate, hidden coves, the island offers a variety of beach experiences to suit every traveler. Whether you're a sunbather seeking the perfect spot to relax, an adrenaline junkie looking to ride the waves, or a family in search of safe, fun waters, Fuerteventura delivers on every front.

In addition to its stunning beaches, Fuerteventura is also a haven for watersports enthusiasts. The island's year-round sunshine, steady winds, and clear waters create perfect conditions for surfing, windsurfing, kitesurfing, snorkeling, and diving. Whether you're an experienced pro or a complete beginner, there's an opportunity to get out on the water and experience the thrill of the ocean.

In this chapter, we'll take you through the best beaches for sunbathing, the top spots for surfing and wind sports, and where to go for diving, snorkeling, and family-friendly beach fun. Whatever your beach day dream looks like, Fuerteventura has something for you.

Best Beaches for Sunbathing

Fuerteventura's beaches are tailor-made for sunbathing, with their soft sands, expansive shores, and tranquil atmospheres. Whether you're looking for a lively beach with amenities or a quiet, secluded spot to escape the crowds, you'll find the perfect place to relax and soak up the island's famous sunshine.

- **Playa de Sotavento (Jandía Peninsula)**

    Playa de Sotavento, located on the Jandía Peninsula, is often considered one of the most stunning beaches in Fuerteventura. Its five-kilometer stretch of golden sand and shallow turquoise waters make it an ideal spot for sunbathers looking for a tranquil day by the sea. The beach's size means you'll always find a peaceful spot to lay out your towel, even in the height of summer.

    Sotavento is famous for its sandbanks and lagoons that form at low tide, creating natural pools perfect for lounging in the water without being buffeted by waves. It's an incredibly photogenic beach, with the contrast of the sand, sea, and sky creating a scene straight out of a postcard. There are few facilities along the beach, so bring your own food, drinks, and umbrella for shade.

- **Playa de Cofete (Jandía Peninsula)**

    If you're seeking solitude and untouched beauty, **Playa de Cofete** is the ultimate sunbathing destination. Located on the remote western side of the Jandía Peninsula, this 12-kilometer beach is known for its wild, rugged beauty and sense of isolation. It's not uncommon to find yourself completely alone here, with nothing but the sound of the waves and the wind.

The beach is backed by the towering **Jandía Mountains**, adding to its dramatic atmosphere. While the rough currents and strong winds make swimming dangerous, Cofete is perfect for sunbathing, long walks, and simply enjoying the raw beauty of nature. There are no facilities at Cofete, and it's best reached by 4x4, so be sure to come prepared with everything you'll need for the day.

- **Playa de La Concha (El Cotillo)**

For a more relaxed sunbathing experience, head to **Playa de La Concha** near **El Cotillo** on the northwest coast. This crescent-shaped beach is sheltered by natural rock formations, creating calm, shallow waters that are perfect for swimming and floating. The beach's soft white sand is ideal for sunbathing, and its relatively quiet atmosphere makes it a favorite among locals and visitors who prefer a more laid-back vibe.

There are a few beach bars and restaurants nearby, so you won't need to venture far if you're in the mood for a cold drink or a light snack. The sunsets here are particularly beautiful, making it a great spot to stay until evening and watch the sun dip below the horizon.

- **Playa de Grandes Playas (Corralejo Natural Park)**

Grandes Playas, located within **Corralejo Natural Park**, is a series of wide, sandy beaches that stretch along the northeast coast of the island. This area is perfect for sunbathers who love vast, open spaces and stunning views. The beaches here are backed by the famous sand dunes of Corralejo, giving you a unique landscape to enjoy while you relax on the sand.

The water is usually calm enough for swimming, though the winds can pick up, making it a favorite for windsurfers and kitesurfers further along the beach. The size of Grandes Playas means it never feels crowded, and there are several spots along the beach with sunbeds and umbrellas available for rent.

Surfing, Windsurfing, and Kitesurfing Hotspots

Fuerteventura is internationally renowned as a top destination for water sports, particularly surfing, windsurfing, and kitesurfing. Thanks to its consistent trade winds and a variety of beach conditions, the island attracts enthusiasts from around the globe. Whether you're a seasoned rider or looking to take your first lesson, Fuerteventura offers some of the best conditions in Europe.

- **El Cotillo** (Northwest)

  The laid-back town of **El Cotillo** is a surfer's paradise, with several beaches offering perfect waves for both beginners and experienced surfers. The main surf spot, **Playa del Castillo**, features consistent waves year-round, with several surf schools located nearby that cater to all skill levels. The beach's mellow vibe and stunning surroundings make it a favorite among surfers looking to escape the busier beaches in the north.

If you're new to surfing, there are several beginner-friendly breaks near **El Cotillo** where you can get your first taste of riding the waves. The surf schools in the area offer group and private lessons, as well as board and wetsuit rentals, so you'll have everything you need to get started.

- **Flag Beach (Corralejo)**

Known as one of the best spots for both kitesurfing and windsurfing, **Flag Beach** in Corralejo is a hotspot for water sports enthusiasts. The steady winds and consistent waves make it ideal for intermediate and advanced riders, but it's also a great place for beginners, thanks to the local surf and kite schools that offer lessons and equipment rental.

The beach is long and wide, giving kitesurfers and windsurfers plenty of space to launch and ride without feeling crowded. The wind here is most reliable from April to September, but you can find riders out on the water year-round. The atmosphere at Flag Beach is friendly and welcoming, with a lively kitesurfing community that's always happy to share tips with newcomers.

- **Sotavento Beach (Jandía Peninsula)**

Sotavento Beach is one of the world's most famous windsurfing and kitesurfing spots, attracting professionals and amateurs alike. The beach's unique sandbars and shallow lagoons create ideal conditions for learning, while the offshore winds provide the perfect challenge for more experienced riders.

Sotavento regularly hosts the **Windsurfing and Kiteboarding World Cup**, making it a hub for water sports enthusiasts during the competition season. If you're new to the sport, there are several schools along the beach offering lessons and equipment rental. The calm waters of the lagoons are perfect for practicing your skills before heading out into the open sea.

- **Playa de Esquinzo (Northwest)**

    If you're an experienced surfer looking for a more challenging wave, **Playa de Esquinzo** on the northwest coast is a hidden gem that offers powerful, consistent surf. The beach is less crowded than some of the more popular surf spots, and its rugged beauty makes it a favorite among those in the know.

    The waves at Esquinzo can get big, especially during the winter months, so it's best suited for intermediate to advanced surfers. The beach is relatively isolated, so bring your own equipment and provisions if you plan to spend the day chasing waves.

Diving and Snorkeling Locations

While Fuerteventura is often associated with its above-water sports, its underwater world is just as thrilling. The island's clear waters, volcanic reefs, and abundant marine life make it an excellent destination for snorkeling and diving. Whether you're exploring shallow lagoons or diving deep to discover shipwrecks and volcanic caves, there's an underwater adventure waiting for you.

- **Isla de Lobos** (Near Corralejo)

  Just a short boat ride from Corralejo lies **Isla de Lobos**, a small, uninhabited island that's part of a protected marine reserve. The waters around Isla de Lobos are some of the clearest in Fuerteventura, making it a popular spot for snorkeling and diving. The island's sheltered bays are home to a variety of marine life, including colorful fish, rays, and even octopuses.

  Snorkelers can enjoy exploring the shallow waters near **Playa de La Concha**, where the calm sea provides excellent visibility and a chance to spot schools of fish swimming around the volcanic rock formations. For divers, the deeper waters around the island offer more challenging sites, including underwater caves and reefs teeming with marine life.

- **Caleta de Fuste** (East Coast)

  The calm, sheltered bay of **Caleta de Fuste** is an ideal spot for beginner snorkelers and divers. The water here is shallow and clear, making it easy to see a variety of fish and marine creatures up close. The bay's natural breakwater protects it from strong currents, creating a safe and relaxing environment for those new to snorkeling or diving.

Several dive schools in Caleta de Fuste offer courses and guided dives for all experience levels, so whether you're looking to earn your certification or just enjoy a casual dive, you'll find plenty of options here.

- **Las Salinas (South of Caleta de Fuste)**

For a more off-the-beaten-path diving experience, head to **Las Salinas**, just south of Caleta de Fuste. This area is home to several dive sites that feature volcanic reefs, shipwrecks, and a wide variety of marine life, including eels, rays, and groupers. The **SS American Star** wreck, which has mostly disappeared into the sea, can still be explored by experienced divers in this area.

The underwater terrain at Las Salinas is fascinating, with volcanic rock formations and caves providing plenty of nooks and crannies to explore. The local dive centers offer guided tours of the wrecks and reefs, making it a great spot for adventurous divers looking to discover something new.

Family-Friendly Beaches and Activities

Fuerteventura is a fantastic destination for families, with its safe beaches, shallow waters, and range of activities that appeal to kids and adults alike. Whether you're looking for a beach with calm waters for swimming or fun, family-friendly activities like snorkeling or kayaking, the island has plenty to offer.

- **Playa de Costa Calma (Jandía Peninsula)**

    Playa de Costa Calma is a great choice for families, thanks to its calm, shallow waters and wide, sandy beach. The beach is perfect for young children to splash around in, and there are plenty of sunbeds and umbrellas available for rent, so parents can relax while keeping an eye on the kids. There are also several restaurants and cafes nearby, making it easy to grab a bite to eat without leaving the beach.

    The beach's calm conditions also make it ideal for beginners looking to try their hand at snorkeling or paddleboarding. Several watersports centers along the beach offer rentals and lessons for families looking to add a bit of adventure to their day.

- **Playa de La Concha (El Cotillo)**

    As one of the island's most sheltered beaches, **Playa de La Concha** is perfect for families with young children. The natural rock formations create a series of small, shallow lagoons where kids can safely play in the water without worrying about strong waves. The beach is quiet and relaxed, with soft sand that's ideal for building sandcastles.

Playa de La Concha also offers great snorkeling opportunities for families. The calm waters are filled with colorful fish, and the beach's proximity to El Cotillo means you'll find plenty of nearby restaurants and amenities.

- **Playa Chica (Puerto del Rosario)**

For a more urban beach experience, **Playa Chica** in Puerto del Rosario is a small, family-friendly beach that offers calm waters and plenty of facilities. Located in the island's capital, Playa Chica is easily accessible and features a playground, showers, and a nearby cafe, making it a convenient choice for families staying in the city.

The beach's shallow waters are perfect for swimming, and its central location means you can combine a beach day with a visit to some of Puerto del Rosario's other attractions, such as the local shops and markets.

- **Oasis Park Fuerteventura (La Lajita)**

While not a beach, **Oasis Park** in **La Lajita** is a must-visit for families looking for a fun day out. This large wildlife park and botanical garden is home to over 3,000 animals, including giraffes, elephants, and sea lions, and offers a variety of interactive experiences, such as camel rides and animal feedings.

The park also features several water-based attractions, including a sea lion show and a chance to splash around in the water play areas. It's a great way to break up your beach days with a bit of adventure and education for the whole family.

Conclusion

Whether you're looking for a relaxing day of sunbathing, an adrenaline-fueled watersports adventure, or a family-friendly beach outing, Fuerteventura's beaches and watersports offer something for everyone. From the windswept shores of Sotavento to the tranquil lagoons of El Cotillo, the island's diverse coastline promises unforgettable experiences, no matter your beach style. Dive into the waves, explore the underwater world, or simply bask in the sun—Fuerteventura's beaches are waiting for you.

Outdoor Adventures in Fuerteventura

While Fuerteventura is often associated with its pristine beaches and water sports, the island's rugged interior and unique landscapes offer a playground for outdoor enthusiasts of all kinds. From hiking across volcanic craters and cycling along coastal paths to watching rare birds in nature reserves, Fuerteventura is a paradise for adventurers who want to experience the island's raw, untamed beauty up close. Its dramatic terrain, shaped by volcanic activity millions of years ago, is home to fascinating ecosystems, panoramic viewpoints, and peaceful rural villages that reveal a side of the island many visitors overlook.

This chapter will take you through the best outdoor adventures Fuerteventura has to offer, including hiking trails, cycling routes, volcano explorations, and wildlife watching. Whether you're a seasoned adventurer or a casual nature lover, these experiences will give you a deeper connection to Fuerteventura's natural beauty and diverse landscapes.

Hiking Trails and Nature Walks

Fuerteventura's varied terrain, from rolling sand dunes to jagged volcanic peaks, provides a wide range of hiking opportunities for all levels. Whether you're looking for a challenging trek to the island's highest summit or a leisurely nature walk through peaceful valleys, Fuerteventura's trails allow you to explore the island's wild side at your own pace.

- **Pico de la Zarza (Jandía Peninsula)**

If you're an experienced hiker looking for a rewarding challenge, the hike to **Pico de la Zarza** is one of the most spectacular on the island. As the highest point in Fuerteventura, Pico de la Zarza stands at 807 meters (2,648 feet) and offers breathtaking panoramic views of the **Jandía Peninsula**, including the beaches of **Cofete** and **Playa de Sotavento**.

The trail to the summit begins near **Morro Jable** and takes about 3 to 4 hours to reach the top, depending on your fitness level. The hike is steep and challenging, but the effort is well worth it once you reach the summit and take in the sweeping views of the island's southern coastline and rugged interior. The path is well-marked, but be sure to bring plenty of water, sun protection, and good hiking shoes, as the trail can be rocky and exposed to the elements.

- **Montaña de Tindaya (Tindaya)**

Montaña de Tindaya is one of the most sacred mountains on the island, revered by the island's indigenous **Majo** people. Located near the village of **Tindaya**, this volcanic mountain offers a moderate hike with incredible views of Fuerteventura's northwestern plains and coastline.

The hike to the summit of Montaña de Tindaya is relatively short, taking about 1 to 1.5 hours, but the experience is deeply rewarding. As you ascend, you'll notice ancient petroglyphs carved into the rocks, believed to have been left by the Majos as part of religious rituals. Once at the top, you'll have a 360-degree view of the island, including the nearby **Isla de Lobos** and **Lanzarote**. The hike is best attempted in the early morning or late afternoon to avoid the midday heat.

- **Barranco de las Peñitas (Betancuria Rural Park)**

For a more relaxed hike that takes you through one of the island's most picturesque areas, the **Barranco de las Peñitas** is a must-do. This scenic valley, located within the **Betancuria Rural Park**, is home to lush palm groves, dramatic rock formations, and a small, peaceful reservoir that creates a surprising oasis in Fuerteventura's arid landscape.

The trail is relatively easy and suitable for all fitness levels, making it a great option for families or those looking for a leisurely walk. Along the way, you'll pass by the **Ermita de la Peña**, a small chapel dedicated to the island's patron saint, **Nuestra Señora de la Peña**. The combination of natural beauty, wildlife, and local history makes this hike a well-rounded outdoor adventure.

- **Calderón Hondo (Lajares)**

If you're fascinated by Fuerteventura's volcanic history, the hike to the top of **Calderón Hondo** offers a chance to peer into one of the island's best-preserved volcanic craters. Located near the village of **Lajares**, Calderón Hondo is an extinct volcano that provides a relatively easy hike with incredible views of the surrounding volcanic landscape.

The trail takes about 45 minutes to an hour to reach the crater's rim, where you'll be rewarded with stunning views down into the crater itself, as well as panoramic vistas of northern Fuerteventura. On clear days, you can even see across the ocean to the neighboring island of **Lanzarote**. The trail is well-marked and accessible, making it a great option for hikers of all ages.

Cycling Routes Across the Island

Fuerteventura's quiet roads, smooth terrain, and beautiful scenery make it an ideal destination for cycling enthusiasts. Whether you're a road cyclist looking to cover long distances or a mountain biker seeking rugged off-road trails, the island offers a variety of routes that showcase its stunning landscapes. With its relatively flat terrain in many areas and low traffic, Fuerteventura provides cyclists with plenty of opportunities to explore at their own pace.

- **Corralejo to El Cotillo (North Coast)**

  One of the most scenic cycling routes on the island is the coastal ride from **Corralejo** to **El Cotillo**. This route takes you along the north coast, offering stunning views of the Atlantic Ocean, rolling sand dunes, and volcanic terrain. The ride is about 20 kilometers one way and is relatively flat, making it suitable for both beginner and intermediate cyclists.

Along the way, you'll pass through the **Corralejo Natural Park**, where you can stop to explore the dunes or take a dip in the ocean. The route also passes by several quiet beaches, including **Playa de Majanicho**, where you can rest and enjoy the peaceful surroundings. Once you reach El Cotillo, you can relax at one of the village's beachside cafes or explore its famous lagoons.

- **La Pared to Costa Calma (Jandía Peninsula)**

For a more challenging route, the ride from **La Pared** to **Costa Calma** on the Jandía Peninsula offers a mix of road and off-road cycling through Fuerteventura's southern landscapes. The ride covers about 25 kilometers and takes you through rugged desert terrain, with occasional climbs that offer panoramic views of the coastline.

This route is perfect for cyclists who enjoy a bit of adventure, as it includes sections of dirt tracks and rocky paths. Along the way, you'll have the chance to see some of the island's lesser-known beaches, such as **Playa de Viejo Rey**, which is popular with surfers. The ride ends in Costa Calma, where you can reward yourself with a swim in the calm waters of **Playa de Costa Calma**.

- **Betancuria Circuit (Central Fuerteventura)**

    If you're looking for a more challenging road cycling route, the **Betancuria Circuit** offers a tough but rewarding ride through Fuerteventura's mountainous interior. Starting in the historic town of **Betancuria**, the route covers about 40 kilometers and includes several steep climbs and descents.

    The road winds through volcanic peaks, scenic valleys, and quiet rural villages, offering stunning views of the island's rugged landscape. The highlight of the route is the climb to the **Mirador de Morro Velosa**, a viewpoint designed by the famous Canarian artist **César Manrique**, where you can take in sweeping views of Fuerteventura's interior.

Exploring Volcanoes and Lava Fields

Fuerteventura's volcanic origins are evident everywhere you look, from the jagged peaks that dominate the skyline to the barren lava fields that stretch across the island. Exploring these volcanic landscapes is a fascinating way to connect with Fuerteventura's geological history and experience its otherworldly beauty.

- **Montaña Roja (Corralejo)**

    Montaña Roja, or **Red Mountain**, is an extinct volcano located just south of Corralejo. The hike to its summit is a relatively short but steep climb that offers fantastic views of the **Corralejo Natural Park**, the nearby **Isla de Lobos**, and the island of **Lanzarote**. The red hue of the volcanic rock contrasts beautifully with the white sand dunes and the blue ocean, creating a stunning visual experience.

The hike takes about 45 minutes to an hour, and while it's not overly strenuous, it's best to attempt it in the cooler parts of the day. From the summit, you'll be able to see the full expanse of Fuerteventura's northern coast, making it a perfect spot for photography or simply enjoying the breathtaking views.

- **Malpaís de la Arena (La Oliva)**

The **Malpaís de la Arena** is a large volcanic field located near the town of **La Oliva**, where you can explore a surreal landscape of solidified lava flows and volcanic craters. This area was formed during a volcanic eruption over 10,000 years ago, and it remains one of the most geologically significant sites on the island.

The hike through the lava fields takes you across rugged terrain, past ancient craters and black lava rock formations. It's a relatively easy walk, but the lack of shade and the rough ground make it important to bring plenty of water and wear sturdy shoes. The **Caldera de la Arena** is the main attraction, and the views from its rim offer a unique perspective on Fuerteventura's volcanic past.

Wildlife Watching and Birding

Fuerteventura's unique ecosystems, from its coastal wetlands to its arid plains, provide a habitat for a wide variety of wildlife, particularly birds. The island is home to several important nature reserves and birdwatching areas where you can spot both resident and migratory species, making it a great destination for nature lovers and birding enthusiasts.

- **Salinas del Carmen (East Coast)**

    The **Salinas del Carmen**, located on the east coast near **Caleta de Fuste**, is one of the best places on the island for birdwatching. These salt flats and wetlands attract a variety of bird species, particularly during the winter months when migratory birds stop here on their journey between Europe and Africa.

    Common species you might spot include **Kentish plovers**, **little egrets**, and **grey herons**. The area is peaceful and relatively quiet, making it an ideal spot for watching birds without the crowds. There's also a small museum nearby, the **Museo de la Sal**, where you can learn about the history of salt production in Fuerteventura.

- **Isla de Lobos (Near Corralejo)**

    Isla de Lobos is a small, uninhabited island located just off the coast of Corralejo. It's a designated nature reserve and a popular spot for wildlife watching, particularly birds. The island's diverse habitats, including its rocky shores, lagoons, and salt marshes, provide a haven for both resident and migratory bird species.

Some of the birds you might see on Isla de Lobos include **ospreys**, **yellow-legged gulls**, and various wading birds. The island is also home to a variety of marine life, and you may spot dolphins or sea turtles in the waters surrounding the island.

- **Jandía Natural Park (Jandía Peninsula)**

The **Jandía Natural Park** is one of the most important wildlife areas on the island, particularly for birdwatching. The park's diverse landscapes, including its mountains, valleys, and coastal areas, provide a habitat for a wide variety of species, including the rare **Canary Islands stonechat**, which is endemic to Fuerteventura.

Other species you might encounter in the park include **Barbary falcons**, **hoopoes**, and various species of larks and finches. The park's remote location and rugged terrain make it a perfect place for wildlife enthusiasts to explore, and the lack of human development means the area remains largely undisturbed.

Conclusion

Fuerteventura's outdoor adventures offer a diverse range of experiences for nature lovers, adventurers, and wildlife enthusiasts alike. Whether you're hiking to the island's highest peak, cycling through its volcanic landscape, or watching rare birds in its nature reserves, Fuerteventura provides endless opportunities to connect with its stunning natural environment. The island's wild beauty, shaped by millions of years of volcanic activity and erosion, is waiting to be discovered by those willing to venture beyond its beaches and into its rugged interior.

Cultural Experiences in Fuerteventura

While Fuerteventura may be known for its stunning beaches and outdoor adventures, the island's rich cultural heritage offers visitors a deeper, more intimate connection to its soul. This is an island where ancient traditions are still honored, where local festivals light up quiet towns, and where every meal is a celebration of fresh, local ingredients. From traditional music and art to vibrant local festivals, Fuerteventura has a culture deeply rooted in its unique history and the rhythms of the ocean and land.

In this chapter, we'll dive into the cultural experiences that make Fuerteventura so special, from its lively festivals and delicious cuisine to its museums, cultural centers, and thriving arts scene. Whether you're looking to immerse yourself in local traditions or simply enjoy a great meal, this guide will help you discover the island's authentic cultural heart.

Traditional Festivals and Events

Fuerteventura's calendar is filled with festivals and events that celebrate the island's heritage, religion, and agricultural traditions. These festivals often bring entire communities together in joyful celebration, and visitors are always welcome to join in the fun. Whether it's a religious procession, a harvest festival, or a music and dance performance, experiencing a local festival is a great way to connect with the island's traditions and spirit.

- **Fiesta de Nuestra Señora de la Peña (Betancuria)**

    One of the most important festivals on the island is the **Fiesta de Nuestra Señora de la Peña**, held every September in honor of **Nuestra Señora de la Peña**, the patron saint of Fuerteventura. This religious festival takes place in **Betancuria**, the island's former capital and spiritual heart, and attracts thousands of pilgrims from across Fuerteventura and the other Canary Islands.

    The festival includes a pilgrimage to the **Ermita de la Peña**, a small chapel dedicated to the Virgin, followed by a series of religious ceremonies, processions, and lively celebrations. Locals and visitors alike gather to pay their respects, enjoy traditional music and dance, and share meals with family and friends. The atmosphere is one of reverence, community, and joy, making it a memorable experience for those lucky enough to attend.

- **Carnival (Across the Island)**

    Like much of Spain, Fuerteventura celebrates **Carnival** in the weeks leading up to Lent, and the festivities are some of the liveliest and most colorful on the island. Carnival in Fuerteventura is celebrated in towns and villages across the island, with each location putting its own unique spin on the event. The biggest and most extravagant celebrations take place in **Puerto del Rosario**, **Corralejo**, and **Morro Jable**, where you'll find parades, music, dancing, and costumes that range from the outrageous to the downright surreal.

The highlight of Carnival is the **Gran Cabalgata**, a massive parade where floats, dancers, and musicians fill the streets with music and color. The event culminates in the **Entierro de la Sardina** (Burial of the Sardine), a traditional Canarian ritual where a giant papier-mâché sardine is paraded through the streets before being set on fire in a symbolic farewell to the excesses of Carnival. The energy, fun, and community spirit of Carnival make it one of the island's most anticipated events.

- **Feria Insular de Artesanía (Antigua)**

If you're interested in Fuerteventura's artisan traditions, the **Feria Insular de Artesanía**, held annually in **Antigua**, is a must-visit. This craft fair is the largest on the island and attracts artisans from across the Canary Islands to showcase their handmade goods, from pottery and textiles to jewelry and woodwork. The fair is a celebration of traditional Canarian crafts, many of which have been passed down through generations.

In addition to the stalls selling crafts, the fair features live demonstrations, where you can watch artisans at work and learn about the traditional techniques used to create their products. There are also food stalls offering local delicacies, traditional music and dance performances, and workshops for those who want to try their hand at making their own crafts. The Feria Insular de Artesanía is a great opportunity to experience Fuerteventura's rich cultural heritage and take home a unique souvenir.

- **Día de Canarias (Canary Islands Day)**

    Celebrated every year on **May 30th, Día de Canarias** marks the anniversary of the establishment of the Canary Islands' autonomous government in 1983. On this day, the entire archipelago comes alive with celebrations of Canarian culture, and Fuerteventura is no exception. Towns and villages across the island host events that showcase traditional Canarian music, dance, and food, with locals dressing in traditional attire and participating in cultural performances.

    In Fuerteventura, **Puerto del Rosario** is the center of many of the Día de Canarias celebrations, with concerts, folk dancing, and street parties that last well into the night. It's a fantastic opportunity for visitors to experience the island's cultural pride and enjoy the warm, welcoming atmosphere of a local fiesta.

Local Cuisine and Dining Guide

Fuerteventura's cuisine is a reflection of its land, sea, and agricultural traditions, with simple, flavorful dishes that showcase the island's fresh ingredients. Whether you're dining in a small village tavern or a beachside restaurant, you'll find that the island's food is rooted in local produce, fresh seafood, and the famous **Queso Majorero**, a unique goat cheese made from the milk of the island's native goats.

- **Papas Arrugadas con Mojo**

One of the most iconic dishes in the Canary Islands, and a must-try in Fuerteventura, is **papas arrugadas con mojo**. These are small, wrinkled potatoes that are boiled in heavily salted water and served with **mojo rojo** (a spicy red sauce made with peppers and paprika) or **mojo verde** (a green sauce made with cilantro and garlic). This dish is a staple on every local menu and is often served as a side dish or tapa.

- **Fresh Seafood**

Given Fuerteventura's location in the Atlantic Ocean, seafood plays a central role in the island's cuisine. You'll find fresh fish such as **vieja** (parrotfish), **cherne** (grouper), and **sama** (bream) on many menus, often grilled simply with olive oil and garlic. Other seafood dishes to try include **pulpo a la gallega** (Galician-style octopus), **calamares a la romana** (fried squid), and **gambas al ajillo** (garlic prawns).

Many of the best seafood restaurants are located in the island's coastal towns and fishing villages, such as **El Cotillo**, **Ajuy**, and **Morro Jable**, where you can enjoy your meal with a view of the ocean.

- **Queso Majorero**

Fuerteventura is famous for its **Queso Majorero**, a goat cheese made from the milk of the island's indigenous

Majorera goats. This cheese has a distinct flavor, which varies depending on how long it's aged, and can be enjoyed in a variety of forms—fresh, semi-cured, or cured. It's often served as a tapa, drizzled with honey or paired with local wine.

You can sample Queso Majorero at restaurants across the island, or visit local farms and dairies to learn more about the cheese-making process and buy it directly from the producers. The **Feria del Queso**, held annually in **Antigua**, is a great opportunity to taste a variety of cheeses from local producers.

- **Gofio**
  Gofio is a traditional Canarian flour made from roasted grains, typically wheat or corn, and it has been a staple of the Canarian diet for centuries. In Fuerteventura, gofio is often mixed with water, milk, or honey to create a simple, nutritious dish. You'll find gofio used in a variety of dishes, from soups and stews to desserts like **mousse de gofio**.

- **Where to Eat**

Fuerteventura offers a wide range of dining experiences, from casual beachside cafes to fine dining restaurants. Some of the best places to enjoy local cuisine include:

  - **Casa Santa María (Betancuria)**: Located in the historic town of Betancuria, this charming restaurant offers a menu of traditional Canarian

dishes made with local ingredients. The restaurant's rustic, colonial-style decor adds to the authentic dining experience.
- **La Vaca Azul (El Cotillo)**: A favorite among locals and visitors alike, this seafood restaurant in the fishing village of El Cotillo serves up some of the freshest fish on the island, with stunning views of the Atlantic Ocean.
- **Casa Marcos (Villaverde)**: Known for its creative take on traditional Canarian cuisine, **Casa Marcos** offers a menu that changes with the seasons, featuring dishes made from locally sourced ingredients. Don't miss their goat cheese with palm honey or grilled octopus.
- **El Horno (La Oliva)**: A family-run restaurant in the village of La Oliva, **El Horno** specializes in grilled meats and traditional Canarian dishes. The warm, welcoming atmosphere makes it a great place to experience local hospitality.

Museums and Cultural Centers

Fuerteventura may be known for its natural beauty, but the island also has a rich cultural heritage that is preserved and celebrated in its museums and cultural centers. These institutions offer a fascinating insight into the island's history, from its indigenous roots to its colonial past and beyond.

- **Museo Arqueológico de Betancuria**

  Located in the island's former capital, the **Museo Arqueológico de Betancuria** is one of the best places to learn about Fuerteventura's ancient history. The museum houses a collection of artifacts from the island's pre-Hispanic period, including tools, pottery, and religious objects left behind by the indigenous **Majo** people.

  The exhibits provide a glimpse into the daily lives of the Majos, their agricultural practices, and their spiritual beliefs. The museum also explores the impact of the Spanish conquest on the island's indigenous population, offering a deeper understanding of Fuerteventura's cultural history.

- **Centro de Arte Canario (La Oliva)**

  The **Centro de Arte Canario** in **La Oliva** is a cultural center dedicated to contemporary Canarian art. The center features a rotating collection of works by local artists, as well as permanent exhibitions that showcase the art and culture of the Canary Islands. The gallery's focus on modern art provides an interesting contrast to Fuerteventura's more traditional cultural offerings.

  In addition to the art exhibitions, the center hosts workshops, cultural events, and performances throughout the year, making it a lively hub for the local arts community.

- **Ecomuseo de La Alcogida (Tefía)**

  For a glimpse into Fuerteventura's rural past, the **Ecomuseo de La Alcogida** in **Tefía** is a fascinating open-air museum that recreates traditional village life on the island. The museum consists of a group of restored houses, each showcasing different aspects of rural life, from agriculture and goat herding to traditional crafts like pottery and weaving.

  Visitors can explore the houses and watch live demonstrations of traditional skills, such as bread-making and cheese production. It's a great way to experience the island's agricultural heritage and learn more about the daily lives of Fuerteventura's rural communities in the past.

Art, Music, and Performances

Fuerteventura's artistic and musical traditions are deeply intertwined with its history and culture, and the island's art scene continues to thrive today. From traditional folk music and dance to modern art and performances, there are plenty of ways to experience Fuerteventura's creative spirit.

- **Folklore and Traditional Music**

  Traditional **Canarian folk music** is an important part of Fuerteventura's cultural identity, and you'll often hear it at local festivals and events. The music typically features instruments like the **timple** (a small five-stringed guitar), guitars, and drums, accompanied by lively singing and dancing. The songs often tell stories of rural life, love, and the island's natural beauty.

One of the best ways to experience traditional Canarian music is to attend a **romería**, a religious procession that often features music, dancing, and local food. These events are held in towns and villages across the island throughout the year, especially during local fiestas and religious festivals.

- **Cultural Performances and Festivals**

Throughout the year, Fuerteventura hosts a variety of cultural performances and festivals that showcase the island's artistic talent. The **Festival Internacional de Cometas** (International Kite Festival) in Corralejo is one of the island's most visually spectacular events, where artists and kite enthusiasts from around the world gather to create elaborate kite displays over the sand dunes.

The **Fuerteventura en Música** festival, held every summer in **El Cotillo**, is a popular music event that features a mix of Canarian, Spanish, and international artists performing a wide range of genres, from folk and rock to world music. The festival takes place on the beach, creating a relaxed, open-air atmosphere that's perfect for enjoying live music.

- **Local Art and Galleries**

Fuerteventura is home to a growing community of artists, many of whom draw inspiration from the island's natural beauty and cultural traditions. In addition to the **Centro de Arte Canario** in La Oliva, you'll find several smaller galleries and studios across the island where local artists display their work.

In the village of **Lajares**, for example, there's a thriving arts scene, with several galleries showcasing contemporary art, ceramics, and handmade crafts. The **Mercado Artesanal** in Lajares, held every Saturday, is a great place to meet local artists, browse their creations, and pick up unique pieces to take home.

Conclusion

Fuerteventura's cultural experiences offer a rich and diverse journey into the heart of the island. Whether you're taking part in a lively festival, savoring the local cuisine, exploring a museum, or enjoying traditional music and art, the island's vibrant cultural life adds depth and meaning to your visit. By embracing Fuerteventura's traditions, stories, and creative spirit, you'll discover a side of the island that goes beyond its beaches and landscapes—one that's rooted in its people, history, and way of life.

Where to Stay in Fuerteventura

Choosing the right place to stay is one of the most important decisions you'll make when visiting Fuerteventura. With its wide variety of accommodations—ranging from luxurious beachfront resorts to budget-friendly apartments and unique eco-lodges—Fuerteventura offers something for every type of traveler. Whether you want to be in the heart of the action, tucked away in a quiet village, or close to nature, this guide will help you find the perfect place to call home during your time on the island.

In this chapter, we'll explore the best resorts and hotels for those seeking comfort and convenience, budget-friendly accommodations for those traveling on a shoestring, unique and eco-friendly stays for those wanting something a little different, and camping and glamping options for the adventurous. No matter your travel style or budget, Fuerteventura has a wide range of options to suit your needs.

Best Resorts and Hotels

If you're looking for a resort experience where you can relax in comfort and enjoy amenities like pools, spas, and restaurants, Fuerteventura has plenty of options to choose from. Many of the island's best resorts are located along its stunning coastlines, offering direct access to beaches, water sports, and spectacular ocean views.

- **Gran Hotel Atlantis Bahía Real (Corralejo)**
  For a luxurious stay in one of Fuerteventura's most

popular areas, the **Gran Hotel Atlantis Bahía Real** in **Corralejo** is hard to beat. This five-star beachfront resort is located just steps from the **Corralejo Natural Park** and its famous sand dunes, offering guests the perfect combination of luxury and natural beauty.

The hotel features spacious rooms and suites, many with ocean views, as well as five on-site restaurants serving a variety of international and Canarian cuisine. There's also a state-of-the-art spa, two outdoor swimming pools, and direct access to a beautiful stretch of beach. The Gran Hotel Atlantis Bahía Real is a great option for couples and families looking for a luxurious and relaxing stay with all the amenities.

- **Sheraton Fuerteventura Beach, Golf & Spa Resort (Caleta de Fuste)**

Located in the popular resort town of **Caleta de Fuste**, the **Sheraton Fuerteventura Beach, Golf & Spa Resort** is a four-star property that offers a wide range of amenities for families and couples alike. The hotel sits right on the beach, with stunning views of the Atlantic Ocean and easy access to local shops, restaurants, and the **Fuerteventura Golf Club**.

The Sheraton features several swimming pools, a full-service spa, and multiple dining options, including both buffet and à la carte restaurants. The spacious rooms are designed with comfort in mind, and many come with balconies or terraces where you can enjoy the ocean breeze. For those traveling with kids, the hotel offers a children's club and family-friendly activities, making it a perfect choice for a relaxing, all-inclusive holiday.

- **Barceló Castillo Beach Resort (Caleta de Fuste)**

Another excellent option in **Caleta de Fuste** is the **Barceló Castillo Beach Resort**, which offers a more casual and laid-back atmosphere while still providing top-notch facilities. The resort is built in the style of a traditional Canarian village, with whitewashed buildings and gardens surrounding a series of swimming pools. It's located right on the beachfront, so you're never far from the sand and sea.

The resort offers a variety of accommodation options, from studios to family-friendly bungalows with kitchenettes, making it a flexible option for both couples and larger groups. With multiple restaurants, a spa, and a marina nearby, the Barceló Castillo Beach Resort is an excellent choice for those who want a convenient, family-friendly beach holiday with plenty of activities.

- **Melia Fuerteventura (Costa Calma)**

Situated on the stunning **Playa de Sotavento** in **Costa Calma**, the **Melia Fuerteventura** is a favorite among water sports enthusiasts, especially kitesurfers and windsurfers. The hotel's prime location on one of the island's most famous beaches offers direct access to the sea, as well as panoramic views of the turquoise lagoons and white sand.

The hotel has several outdoor pools, a spa, and a fitness center, as well as a variety of dining options, including a buffet restaurant and a beach bar. The rooms are modern and stylish, with many offering balconies overlooking the ocean. Melia Fuerteventura is a great option for couples and solo travelers looking to combine relaxation with adventure.

Budget-Friendly Accommodations

Fuerteventura is a fantastic destination for budget travelers, with a wide range of affordable accommodations, from hostels and guesthouses to self-catering apartments. Whether you're traveling solo, as a couple, or with a group of friends, you'll find plenty of budget-friendly options that offer comfort and convenience without breaking the bank.

- **Surf Riders Fuerteventura (Corralejo)**

    Located in the vibrant town of **Corralejo**, **Surf Riders Fuerteventura** is a popular choice for budget-conscious travelers, particularly those interested in surfing or kitesurfing. This laid-back hostel offers both private rooms and dormitory-style accommodation, making it an affordable option for solo travelers or groups.

    Surf Riders features a rooftop terrace with stunning views of the ocean and **Isla de Lobos**, a communal kitchen, and a social lounge where guests can relax and meet fellow travelers. The hostel also organizes surf lessons, excursions, and social events, making it a great place to stay if you're looking for an affordable, fun, and active holiday.

- **Corralejo Surfing Colors Hotel**

Another excellent budget option in **Corralejo** is the **Surfing Colors Hotel**, which offers affordable studio apartments just a short walk from the beach and the town center. The hotel has a relaxed, surf-inspired atmosphere, with a swimming pool, a fitness center, and a bar where guests can unwind after a day of surfing or exploring the island.

Each apartment comes with a kitchenette, allowing you to prepare your own meals and save money on dining out. The central location, combined with the hotel's friendly atmosphere and affordable rates, makes it a great option for budget travelers who want to be close to the action.

- **Casa de los Coroneles (La Oliva)**

For a more traditional and rural experience, consider staying at the **Casa de los Coroneles** in **La Oliva**. This charming guesthouse is set in a historic building that dates back to the 18th century and offers a peaceful retreat in the heart of the countryside.

The rooms are simple but comfortable, with traditional Canarian decor, and the surrounding gardens provide a tranquil atmosphere for relaxing. While Casa de los Coroneles is a bit off the beaten path, it's a great option for those who want to experience the quiet beauty of Fuerteventura's rural villages while staying within a modest budget.

- **Laif Hotel (El Cotillo)**

Laif Hotel, located in the laid-back village of **El Cotillo**, offers a comfortable, budget-friendly stay just minutes from the beach. This small, family-run hotel has a friendly and welcoming atmosphere, with bright, clean rooms and a rooftop terrace that boasts views of the ocean.

The hotel's location in El Cotillo makes it an ideal base for exploring the village's famous lagoons, surfing spots, and local restaurants. It's a great choice for travelers who want a quiet, relaxed stay in one of the island's most picturesque coastal villages without spending a fortune.

Unique Stays: Eco-Lodges, Boutique Hotels, and More

If you're looking for something a little different, Fuerteventura offers a variety of unique accommodations that provide a more personalized and immersive experience. From eco-friendly lodges nestled in the island's volcanic landscapes to charming boutique hotels in historic towns, these stays offer a memorable way to experience the island.

- **Volcano House (Lajares)**

    For those who want to stay close to nature, **Volcano House** in **Lajares** offers a unique and eco-friendly escape. This eco-lodge is built into the volcanic landscape and features sustainable design elements, including solar power, natural materials, and water-saving systems.

    The property is surrounded by volcanic craters and offers stunning views of the island's rugged terrain. Guests can enjoy hiking, cycling, and star-gazing right from their doorstep, and the nearby village of Lajares offers a range of cafes, restaurants, and art galleries. If you're looking for a stay that combines comfort with sustainability, Volcano House is a great option.

- **Viviendas Vacacionales Sol Deluxe (Villaverde)**

    Located in the quiet village of **Villaverde**, **Viviendas Vacacionales Sol Deluxe** offers a collection of boutique villas that provide a peaceful and luxurious retreat. Each villa is beautifully designed with modern furnishings and features a private pool, garden, and terrace with panoramic views of the surrounding countryside.

    The villas are perfect for couples or families looking for privacy and relaxation in a tranquil setting. Villaverde is known for its rural charm and excellent restaurants, and it's a great base for exploring the island's interior and northern beaches.

- **Agroturismo La Gayria (Tiscamanita)**

    For a truly unique experience, consider staying at **Agroturismo La Gayria**, a working farm located in the heart of Fuerteventura's agricultural region. This eco-friendly farmstay offers guests the opportunity to experience rural life firsthand, with accommodations in traditional Canarian houses surrounded by orchards, vineyards, and olive groves.

    Guests can take part in farm activities such as harvesting, cheese-making, and cooking with local ingredients, or simply relax and enjoy the peaceful surroundings. La Gayria is a fantastic option for travelers who want to connect with nature and experience Fuerteventura's rural traditions in an authentic and sustainable way.

Camping and Glamping on the Island

For the adventurous traveler, Fuerteventura offers several opportunities for camping and glamping, allowing you to fully immerse yourself in the island's natural beauty. Whether you're pitching a tent under the stars or staying in a luxurious safari tent, camping in Fuerteventura is a great way to experience the island's stunning landscapes up close.

- **Camping La Rosa de Los Vientos (Corralejo)** Located just outside **Corralejo, Camping La Rosa de Los Vientos** is one of the island's most popular camping sites, offering a variety of options for those who want to experience the great outdoors. The campsite is close to the **Corralejo Natural Park**, giving campers easy access to the island's famous dunes and beaches.

The site offers basic facilities, including showers, toilets, and a communal kitchen, and you can choose to stay in a tent, campervan, or caravan. It's a budget-friendly option for those who want to be close to nature while still being within walking distance of Corralejo's shops, restaurants, and nightlife.

- **Finca de Arrieta (Lanzarote)**

If you're willing to venture to the nearby island of **Lanzarote**, **Finca de Arrieta** offers one of the most unique glamping experiences in the Canary Islands. This eco-friendly retreat is located in the rural north of Lanzarote and features luxurious safari tents, yurts, and stone cottages, all designed with sustainability in mind.

Each accommodation is beautifully furnished and comes with private outdoor space, allowing you to enjoy the stunning volcanic landscapes in comfort. Finca de Arrieta also offers a range of activities, including yoga, surfing, and eco-tours, making it a great option for those looking for a unique and eco-conscious holiday experience.

- **Wild Camping in Fuerteventura**

While wild camping is not officially allowed in most areas of Fuerteventura, there are a few designated camping areas where you can set up camp in a natural setting. **Playa de Cofete**, located on the remote western side of the **Jandía Peninsula**, is a popular spot for those who want to experience wild camping in one of the island's most untouched landscapes.

Be sure to check local regulations and obtain any necessary permits before setting up camp, as restrictions can vary depending on the location. Wild camping offers a truly immersive experience, allowing you to wake up to the sound of the ocean and the sight of the island's rugged beauty all around you.

Conclusion

Whether you're looking for luxury, budget-friendly options, or something more off the beaten path, Fuerteventura offers a diverse range of accommodations to suit every traveler. From the island's best resorts and hotels to eco-lodges, boutique stays, and camping adventures, you'll find a place that feels just right for your journey. No matter where you choose to stay, Fuerteventura's warm hospitality and stunning surroundings will make your visit unforgettable.

Dining and Nightlife in Fuerteventura

Fuerteventura's dining scene is a delightful mix of traditional Canarian flavors, fresh seafood, and international cuisine that reflects the island's diverse cultural influences. Whether you're savoring a meal at a fine dining restaurant, trying out local street food, or enjoying a casual drink at a beachfront bar, the island offers something for every taste and budget. And when the sun sets, Fuerteventura's nightlife comes to life, with its laid-back vibe transforming into lively evenings filled with music, dancing, and laughter.

In this chapter, we'll take you on a culinary and nocturnal journey through the island. We'll highlight the top restaurants where you can experience authentic local cuisine, guide you to the best street food and local delicacies, introduce you to Fuerteventura's nightlife spots, and even suggest where to indulge in wine tasting or sample craft beers from local breweries.

Top Restaurants for Authentic Cuisine

One of the best ways to experience Fuerteventura's culture is through its food. The island's cuisine is simple yet flavorful, relying on fresh, locally sourced ingredients, especially seafood, goat cheese, and traditional Canarian dishes. Here are some of the top restaurants where you can indulge in authentic Fuerteventura cuisine:

- **La Vaca Azul (El Cotillo)**

  Overlooking the picturesque harbor in **El Cotillo**, **La Vaca Azul** is one of the most popular restaurants on the island, known for its fresh seafood and stunning ocean views. The restaurant offers a relaxed, casual atmosphere, where you can enjoy dishes like grilled **vieja** (parrotfish), garlic prawns, and octopus. The seafood is caught fresh daily, and the restaurant's focus on simplicity allows the quality of the ingredients to shine.

  La Vaca Azul's rooftop terrace is the perfect spot for a romantic dinner or a laid-back lunch with friends, offering panoramic views of the Atlantic. Be sure to try the **pulpo a la gallega** (Galician-style octopus) and pair your meal with a glass of local wine for a true Fuerteventura experience.

- **Casa Santa María (Betancuria)**

  Located in the heart of **Betancuria**, Fuerteventura's oldest town, **Casa Santa María** is set in a beautifully restored 17th-century building and offers a menu focused on traditional Canarian cuisine with a modern twist. The restaurant is known for its intimate and elegant atmosphere, perfect for those looking to experience the island's culinary heritage in a refined setting.

  Dishes like **cabrito asado** (roast goat) and **ropa vieja** (shredded beef stew with chickpeas) highlight the island's agricultural and pastoral roots, while the fresh fish and seafood remind you of Fuerteventura's close connection to the sea. Casa Santa María also serves a variety of tapas, and their **queso majorero** (goat cheese) drizzled with palm honey is a must-try.

- **El Horno (La Oliva)**

For an authentic taste of Fuerteventura's rural traditions, head to **El Horno** in the village of **La Oliva**. This family-run restaurant is known for its warm hospitality and traditional dishes, many of which are cooked over an open fire, giving them a rustic, smoky flavor. The restaurant specializes in grilled meats, with the **chuletón de ternera** (beef ribeye) being a standout dish.

El Horno's focus on simple, high-quality ingredients makes it a favorite among locals and visitors alike. The atmosphere is cozy and informal, making it the perfect place to enjoy a relaxed meal with friends or family.

- **Mahoh (Villaverde)**

Mahoh, located in **Villaverde**, is part of a rural hotel and restaurant that offers a unique dining experience in a traditional Canarian farmhouse. The restaurant specializes in using locally sourced ingredients to create a menu that celebrates the flavors of Fuerteventura. The slow-cooked **cabrito (kid goat)** and the fresh **cherne** (grouper) are among the most popular dishes, but the ever-changing seasonal menu ensures there's always something new to try.

The ambiance is rustic and charming, with stone walls and wooden beams creating a warm and inviting setting. Mahoh is also known for its extensive wine list, featuring some of the best Canarian wines to pair with your meal.

Street Food and Local Delicacies

While Fuerteventura is home to some excellent restaurants, you don't need to sit down for a full meal to enjoy the island's flavors. Street food and local delicacies can be found in markets, food stalls, and small cafes, offering a more casual and budget-friendly way to sample traditional Canarian fare.

- **Papas Arrugadas con Mojo**

    One of the most iconic Canarian dishes is **papas arrugadas**, or wrinkled potatoes, served with **mojo** sauce. These small potatoes are boiled in heavily salted water until their skins wrinkle, then served with **mojo rojo** (a spicy red sauce) or **mojo verde** (a green sauce made with cilantro). You can find papas arrugadas in many tapas bars and street food stalls across the island.

    This dish is a favorite among locals and visitors alike, and it's the perfect snack to enjoy while exploring Fuerteventura's markets or enjoying a casual afternoon by the beach.

- **Churros**
    If you're craving something sweet, you'll often find **churros** being sold at local markets and festivals. These

fried dough sticks are served hot and crispy, often dusted with sugar and accompanied by a thick chocolate dipping sauce. Churros are a popular snack, particularly during the island's annual fiestas and fairs.

While they're a simple treat, they're incredibly satisfying, especially when enjoyed with a cup of **café con leche** in the morning or as an indulgent afternoon pick-me-up.

- **Gofio**

Gofio is a traditional Canarian flour made from roasted grains, usually wheat or maize, and has been a staple of the local diet for centuries. You can find gofio in a variety of forms across Fuerteventura, from breakfast cereals and bread to gofio-based desserts like **frangollo** (a sweet pudding made with gofio, milk, sugar, and spices).

In many cafes and bakeries, you can try **gofio mousse**, a light, creamy dessert that pairs the slightly nutty flavor of gofio with a hint of sweetness. It's a unique taste of Fuerteventura's culinary heritage and a must-try for anyone interested in local delicacies.

- **Seafood Tapas**

Fuerteventura's coastal towns are known for their tapas bars, where you can sample small plates of seafood, meats, and local specialties. Popular tapas include **pulpo a la gallega** (octopus with paprika and olive oil), **gambas al ajillo** (garlic prawns), and **calamares a la romana** (fried squid). These tapas are often served with crusty bread and a glass of local wine, making for a perfect light lunch or evening snack.

Tapas bars are also a great way to try a variety of dishes without committing to a full meal. You can order several small plates to share and enjoy a relaxed, social dining experience in a casual setting.

Bars, Clubs, and Nightlife Spots

Fuerteventura's nightlife is as varied as its landscapes. While the island is known for its laid-back vibe, there are still plenty of places to enjoy a lively night out, whether you're looking for a quiet beachfront bar, a bustling pub, or a vibrant nightclub. The island's nightlife is centered in the main towns of **Corralejo**, **Caleta de Fuste**, and **Morro Jable**, but there are also hidden gems to be found in smaller villages and beach towns.

- **Rock Island Bar (Corralejo)**

    A beloved institution in **Corralejo**, **Rock Island Bar** is a live music venue that has been entertaining locals and tourists for over 20 years. Known for its relaxed atmosphere and excellent acoustic performances, Rock Island Bar is the perfect spot to enjoy a drink while listening to talented local and international musicians.

The bar offers a variety of cocktails, beers, and wines, and the friendly staff and cozy setting make it a great place to unwind after a day of exploring the island. The live music typically leans towards acoustic rock, folk, and blues, making it a favorite among music lovers.

- **Waikiki Beach Club (Corralejo)**

If you're looking for a lively night out with beachfront views, **Waikiki Beach Club** in Corralejo is one of the island's most popular spots. During the day, Waikiki operates as a casual beach bar and restaurant, serving fresh seafood and cocktails right on the sand. But by night, it transforms into a vibrant nightclub, with DJs spinning tunes and a dance floor that fills up with both locals and tourists.

The club's open-air design and ocean views create a unique party atmosphere, especially during the summer months when the beach is buzzing with activity. Waikiki Beach Club is the go-to spot for those who want to dance the night away under the stars.

- **Flicks Bar (Corralejo)**

For a fun and quirky night out, head to **Flicks Bar**, a karaoke bar in Corralejo that's known for its lively atmosphere and friendly crowd. Whether you're a karaoke enthusiast or just there to enjoy the show, Flicks is a great place to let loose and have some fun. The bar offers a wide selection of drinks, including cocktails and beers, and the karaoke playlist is extensive, with something for everyone.

Flicks is especially popular with groups, so if you're traveling with friends, it's a great spot to enjoy a fun and casual night out.

- **The Corner House (Caleta de Fuste)**

If you prefer a more low-key evening, **The Corner House** in **Caleta de Fuste** offers a cozy, laid-back pub experience. This British-style pub is a favorite among expats and locals alike, known for its friendly service, extensive drink menu, and live sports broadcasts. The pub also hosts regular quiz nights, live music, and karaoke, making it a lively yet relaxed spot to spend an evening.

- **La Taberna del Blues (Puerto del Rosario)**

For something a bit different, **La Taberna del Blues** in **Puerto del Rosario** is a cozy, intimate bar that specializes in live blues music. The bar has a unique atmosphere, with dim lighting, vintage decor, and a lineup of talented blues musicians performing regularly. Whether you're a fan of the genre or just looking for a relaxed night out with good music, La Taberna del Blues is a hidden gem worth discovering.

Wine Tasting and Local Breweries

While Fuerteventura may not be as well-known for its wine production as some of the other Canary Islands, the island is home to a growing number of vineyards and local breweries that are worth exploring. Wine and beer tasting offer a great way to experience Fuerteventura's local flavors and connect with the island's agricultural heritage.

- **Bodega Conatvs (Tiscamanita)**

    Located in the rural village of **Tiscamanita**, **Bodega Conatvs** is a small, family-run vineyard that produces some of the island's finest wines. The vineyard focuses on organic, sustainable farming practices, and their wines are made from indigenous Canarian grape varieties.

    Visitors can tour the vineyard and winery, learning about the wine-making process and sampling a selection of reds, whites, and rosés. The tasting experience is intimate and personal, with the owners often guiding visitors through the process. It's a great opportunity to taste some truly unique wines and enjoy the peaceful countryside setting.

- **Playita Brewery (Puerto del Rosario)**

For craft beer lovers, **Playita Brewery** in **Puerto del Rosario** is a must-visit. This small, independent brewery produces a range of craft beers, from refreshing pale ales to rich stouts, all brewed using local ingredients and traditional methods.

The brewery offers tours and tastings, where you can sample their beers and learn about the brewing process. Playita Brewery's beers are also available at various bars and restaurants across the island, making it easy to enjoy a local brew during your stay.

- **Finca Canarias Aloe Vera (Lajares)**

   While not a winery or brewery, **Finca Canarias Aloe Vera** in **Lajares** offers a unique tasting experience centered around aloe vera-based products. The farm produces organic aloe vera, which is used in a range of health and beauty products, as well as aloe vera-infused drinks and snacks.

   Visitors can tour the farm, learn about the cultivation of aloe vera, and sample products such as aloe vera juice and aloe-flavored honey. It's a refreshing and unique experience that showcases one of Fuerteventura's most iconic plants.

Conclusion

Fuerteventura's dining and nightlife scene offers a diverse and exciting mix of experiences, from authentic Canarian cuisine and casual street food to vibrant beach clubs and cozy pubs. Whether you're savoring fresh seafood by the ocean, trying your hand at karaoke, or enjoying a glass of local wine under the stars, the island's laid-back yet lively atmosphere ensures there's something for every taste and mood. So, whether you're a foodie, a night owl, or just looking to relax with a drink in hand, Fuerteventura's culinary and social scene will leave you satisfied and eager for more.

Shopping and Souvenirs in Fuerteventura

No trip to Fuerteventura is complete without bringing home a little piece of the island, whether it's a locally made craft, a unique piece of jewelry, or some of the island's famous goat cheese. Fuerteventura's shopping scene offers a mix of modern shopping centers, traditional markets, and local artisan shops where you can find everything from handmade souvenirs to fashion and beauty products. Exploring the island's markets and small stores is not only a great way to support local artisans and businesses but also an opportunity to immerse yourself in the culture and traditions of Fuerteventura.

In this chapter, we'll guide you through the best places to shop on the island, introduce you to Fuerteventura's most distinctive local crafts and artisanal products, and provide a rundown of the island's top markets, where you can find everything from fresh produce to handcrafted souvenirs.

Best Places to Shop

Whether you're looking for a shopping spree at a modern mall or a leisurely stroll through a quaint village filled with boutique stores, Fuerteventura offers a variety of shopping experiences to suit every type of traveler. From major resort areas to smaller villages, here are some of the best places to shop on the island.

- **Las Rotondas Shopping Center (Puerto del Rosario)**

    Located in the island's capital, **Las Rotondas** is Fuerteventura's largest shopping center and the best place to go if you're looking for a modern shopping experience with a wide variety of international brands. The mall features over 100 stores, including popular fashion retailers like **Zara**, **H&M**, **Pull&Bear**, and **Springfield**. You'll also find electronics, beauty products, shoes, and accessories, making it a convenient spot for those who need to pick up essentials during their stay.

Las Rotondas also has several cafes and restaurants, so you can take a break from shopping to enjoy a coffee or a meal. Whether you're looking for fashion, cosmetics, or souvenirs, Las Rotondas is a one-stop destination for all your shopping needs.

- **Calle León y Castillo (Puerto del Rosario)**

Just a short walk from Las Rotondas is **Calle León y Castillo**, one of the main shopping streets in **Puerto del Rosario**. Lined with a mix of high street brands, independent boutiques, and local shops, this street offers a more traditional shopping experience in the heart of the capital. As you stroll down the pedestrian-friendly street, you'll find stores selling everything from clothes and shoes to jewelry, books, and home decor.

Calle León y Castillo is also home to several artisanal and souvenir shops, where you can pick up locally made products, such as ceramics, leather goods, and Canarian crafts. The street is perfect for a relaxed afternoon of shopping, and its central location makes it easy to combine with a visit to one of Puerto del Rosario's nearby museums or cafes.

- **Corralejo Main Street (Corralejo)**

    In the bustling resort town of **Corralejo**, the main shopping area is located along **Avenida Nuestra Señora del Carmen**, a lively street lined with shops, cafes, and restaurants. Corralejo's shops cater to a wide range of tastes, from high-end fashion boutiques to surf shops and souvenir stores.

    For those looking to pick up beachwear or water sports equipment, Corralejo is the place to go. You'll find shops selling everything from surfboards and wetsuits to flip-flops and sunglasses. The street also has several jewelry stores offering handcrafted pieces made from local materials, as well as shops selling artisanal products like hand-painted ceramics, woven baskets, and Canarian embroidery.

- **El Cotillo Village**

    If you prefer a more laid-back, off-the-beaten-path shopping experience, head to the charming village of **El Cotillo** on Fuerteventura's northwest coast. Known for its beautiful beaches and relaxed atmosphere, El Cotillo is also home to several boutique stores and art galleries where you can find one-of-a-kind souvenirs and gifts.

The village has a growing arts community, and many of the shops showcase works by local artists, including paintings, sculptures, and handcrafted jewelry. You'll also find shops selling organic and eco-friendly products, such as handmade soaps, candles, and beauty products made from natural ingredients. El Cotillo is a great place to shop for unique, artisanal items while enjoying the laid-back vibe of this coastal village.

- **Antigua Artisan Shops**

    The village of **Antigua** in the center of the island is known for its traditional architecture and artisan heritage. Here, you'll find several small shops selling locally made crafts, including pottery, woven textiles, and leather goods. The village is also home to the **Museo del Queso Majorero**, where you can learn about Fuerteventura's famous goat cheese and purchase it directly from local producers.

    Antigua is a quiet and charming place to explore, and its artisan shops offer a glimpse into the island's craft traditions. It's a great spot to pick up authentic, handmade souvenirs and support local artisans.

Local Crafts and Artisanal Products

Fuerteventura has a long history of craftsmanship, and the island's artisans continue to produce high-quality, handmade goods that reflect the island's unique culture and natural beauty. From traditional pottery and handwoven textiles to local food products like cheese and honey, Fuerteventura's artisanal offerings make for wonderful souvenirs and gifts.

- **Queso Majorero**

    Queso Majorero is perhaps Fuerteventura's most famous product, and no trip to the island is complete without trying this delicious goat cheese. Made from the milk of the island's native **Majorera** goats, Queso Majorero is known for its rich, creamy flavor and slightly tangy taste. The cheese can be enjoyed fresh, semi-cured, or cured, with the flavor becoming more intense the longer it's aged.

    You can find Queso Majorero in supermarkets, markets, and specialty cheese shops across the island, and it makes for an excellent souvenir to bring home. Many producers also sell vacuum-sealed packages, so you can easily transport the cheese without worrying about it spoiling.

- **Handcrafted Pottery**

    Fuerteventura's pottery tradition dates back to its indigenous **Majo** people, who made clay pots and vessels for everyday use. Today, local artisans continue to create beautiful, hand-painted ceramics that reflect the island's traditional designs and colors. You'll find everything from decorative plates and bowls to vases and figurines, each piece carefully crafted by hand.

Pottery shops and studios can be found in villages like **Antigua**, **Pájara**, and **Betancuria**, where you can purchase these unique pieces directly from the artisans who make them.

- **Leather Goods**

Fuerteventura is home to several talented leatherworkers who create high-quality bags, belts, sandals, and other accessories from locally sourced leather. These handcrafted items make for durable and stylish souvenirs that will remind you of your time on the island. Many leather goods are crafted using traditional techniques, giving them a rustic, artisanal feel.

You can find leather goods in artisan shops across the island, particularly in **Antigua**, **La Oliva**, and **Puerto del Rosario**. Some artisans also offer custom-made pieces, allowing you to design your own unique leather accessory.

- **Canarian Jewelry**

Canarian jewelry is known for its use of natural materials, such as volcanic stones, pearls, and semi-precious gems. Many local jewelers incorporate these materials into their designs, creating pieces that reflect the island's volcanic landscape and ocean surroundings. You'll find necklaces, bracelets, earrings, and rings made from materials like **lava rock**, **olivine** (a green volcanic mineral), and **mother of pearl**.

Local jewelry stores and artisan markets in towns like **Corralejo**, **El Cotillo**, and **Puerto del Rosario** offer a wide selection of handcrafted jewelry, making it easy to find a unique piece that captures the spirit of Fuerteventura.

- **Handwoven Textiles**

Weaving is another traditional craft in Fuerteventura, and local artisans produce beautiful handwoven textiles using natural fibers. You'll find a variety of products, including blankets, rugs, shawls, and table linens, all made with intricate patterns and vibrant colors. These textiles make for beautiful and practical souvenirs that add a touch of Fuerteventura's artisan heritage to your home.

Many weavers use traditional looms and techniques passed down through generations, and you can watch them at work in workshops and artisan shops in villages like **Tefía** and **Antigua**.

- **Aloe Vera Products**

Fuerteventura is known for its **aloe vera** cultivation, and the island's climate makes it an ideal location for growing this healing plant. Aloe vera is used in a wide range of skincare and beauty products, from soothing gels and creams to shampoos and lotions. Local producers harvest the aloe vera by hand and use it to create high-quality, organic products that are free from harsh chemicals.

You can find aloe vera products at specialty shops and farm stores across the island, particularly in **La Oliva** and **Lajares**. Many of these products are made using 100% pure aloe vera, making them a great choice for those looking for natural skincare remedies.

Fuerteventura Markets: What to Buy

Fuerteventura's markets are a treasure trove of local goods, fresh produce, and handmade crafts. Visiting a market is not only a great way to pick up unique souvenirs but also an opportunity to experience the island's vibrant community atmosphere. From weekly farmers' markets to artisan fairs, here are some of the top markets on the island and what to buy when you visit.

- **Mercado de los Tradiciones (La Oliva)**

  Held every Tuesday and Friday in the town of **La Oliva**, the **Mercado de los Tradiciones** (Market of Traditions) is a must-visit for anyone interested in Fuerteventura's artisanal heritage. The market features a variety of stalls selling locally made products, including pottery, jewelry, leather goods, and handwoven textiles. You'll also find fresh produce, such as fruits, vegetables, and goat cheese, as well as baked goods and local honey.

The market has a friendly, welcoming atmosphere, and many of the artisans are happy to chat with visitors about their craft. It's a great place to find unique, handmade souvenirs and support local businesses.

- **Mercado Agrícola de Puerto del Rosario**

If you're looking for fresh, locally grown produce, head to the **Mercado Agrícola** in **Puerto del Rosario**, held every Saturday morning. This farmers' market is the perfect place to stock up on fruits, vegetables, and cheeses, all produced by local farmers. You'll also find stalls selling fresh bread, pastries, and traditional Canarian sweets like **bienmesabe** (a dessert made with almonds, sugar, and lemon).

The market is a great spot to pick up ingredients for a picnic or to try some of Fuerteventura's local delicacies. It's also a wonderful way to experience the island's agricultural traditions and support local farmers.

- **Mercado de la Villa (Antigua)**

The **Mercado de la Villa** in **Antigua** is one of the island's most charming markets, held on the first Sunday of every month. The market features a mix of artisanal goods, fresh produce, and handmade crafts, making it a great place to shop for souvenirs and gifts. You'll find stalls selling everything from handcrafted pottery and leather goods to jewelry, textiles, and aloe vera products.

The market also has a lively atmosphere, with live music and food stalls offering traditional Canarian snacks like **tapas**, **churros**, and **papas arrugadas**. It's a fun and festive place to spend a Sunday morning, and you're sure to leave with some unique finds.

- **El Cotillo Market**

   Held every Friday in the village of **El Cotillo**, this market offers a mix of handmade crafts, jewelry, and art from local artisans. It's a smaller, more intimate market compared to some of the others on the island, but it's a great place to find one-of-a-kind souvenirs and gifts. You'll also find stalls selling organic beauty products, essential oils, and natural soaps.

   The market is held in the main square of El Cotillo, and its relaxed atmosphere makes it a perfect place to browse, chat with artisans, and enjoy the coastal charm of the village.

Conclusion

Shopping in Fuerteventura is a delightful mix of modern convenience and artisanal charm, offering visitors the chance to discover unique, handcrafted products that reflect the island's rich cultural heritage. Whether you're browsing the stalls of a local market, exploring artisan shops in quaint villages, or picking up fresh produce and goat cheese from a farmers' market, Fuerteventura's shopping scene is full of hidden treasures. From pottery and leather goods to aloe vera products and handmade jewelry, the island's crafts and souvenirs provide a lasting connection to your time in this beautiful destination.

Practical Information for Visiting Fuerteventura

Before setting off on your adventure in Fuerteventura, it's essential to arm yourself with some practical information to ensure a smooth and enjoyable trip. While the island is welcoming and laid-back, understanding a bit about health and safety, local customs, money matters, and emergency services can help you feel more confident as you explore this beautiful part of the Canary Islands. From basic health tips and what to expect with local etiquette to banking and emergency contacts, this guide will cover everything you need to know to be well-prepared for your time in Fuerteventura.

Health and Safety Tips

Fuerteventura is generally a very safe and peaceful destination, with low crime rates and a friendly atmosphere. However, as with any trip, it's important to take a few precautions to stay safe and healthy while enjoying all that the island has to offer.

- **Sun Protection**:

    Fuerteventura's sunny climate is one of its main attractions, but the sun can be intense, especially during the summer months. With over 3,000 hours of sunshine annually, it's easy to underestimate the power of the sun, particularly with the island's refreshing trade winds making it feel cooler than it is. Be sure to pack and regularly apply sunscreen with a high SPF, wear a wide-brimmed hat and sunglasses, and seek shade during the hottest part of the day, typically between 12 pm and 3 pm.

Staying hydrated is equally important, so always carry a bottle of water with you, especially if you're hiking or spending the day at the beach. Dehydration can sneak up on you quickly in the hot climate.

- **Swimming Safety**:

Fuerteventura's beaches are stunning, but the island's location in the Atlantic Ocean means that the currents and tides can sometimes be strong, particularly on the west coast. Always check local advice about swimming conditions and look for beaches with lifeguards, especially if you're not a strong swimmer.

Pay attention to the **flag system** at beaches:

- **Green flag**: Safe to swim
- **Yellow flag**: Caution, swim with care
- **Red flag**: Swimming is prohibited, as conditions are dangerous

If you're planning on surfing, windsurfing, or kitesurfing, make sure you understand the local conditions and use equipment that's appropriate for your skill level. Lessons and rentals are widely available for beginners.

- **Medical Services**:

Fuerteventura has modern and reliable healthcare services, with several hospitals and clinics located across the island. The main hospital, **Hospital General de Fuerteventura**, is located in **Puerto del Rosario** and provides emergency care and specialist services. In addition to the hospital, there are smaller medical centers (**Centro de Salud**) in most towns and resort areas.

EU citizens can use their **European Health Insurance Card (EHIC)** or **Global Health Insurance Card (GHIC)** to access medical treatment at public facilities. If you're traveling from outside the EU, make sure you have travel insurance that covers medical expenses in case you need to visit a doctor or hospital.

Pharmacies (**farmacias**) are easily accessible and can provide over-the-counter medications and advice for minor ailments. Look for a green cross sign, which indicates a pharmacy, and note that many pharmacies have alternating hours of operation outside of regular business hours. If you need to find a 24-hour pharmacy, check for a posted sign or ask at your accommodation for assistance.

- **Insect Bites and Stings**:

Fuerteventura is not known for having dangerous insects or wildlife, but it's still a good idea to take precautions against insect bites, particularly mosquitoes. Mosquitoes are more common near the coast and water sources, especially in the warmer months. Using insect repellent and wearing long sleeves in the evening can help reduce bites.

Language and Local Customs

The official language of Fuerteventura, as in the rest of Spain, is **Spanish**, but English and German are widely spoken in tourist areas. While you'll get by just fine with English, especially in resorts, hotels, and restaurants, learning a few basic Spanish phrases will be greatly appreciated by locals and can enhance your travel experience.

- **Basic Spanish Phrases**:
    - **Hola** – Hello
    - **Buenos días** – Good morning
    - **Por favor** – Please
    - **Gracias** – Thank you
    - **¿Cuánto cuesta?** – How much does it cost?
    - **La cuenta, por favor** – The bill, please
    - **¿Dónde está...?** – Where is...?
    - **Perdón** – Excuse me / Sorry

Locals in Fuerteventura tend to be friendly and welcoming, especially if you make an effort to greet them politely. A simple **"Buenos días"** when entering a shop or restaurant is common courtesy.

- **Local Customs**:

The culture in Fuerteventura is a mix of traditional Canarian customs and modern European influences. The island has a slower, more relaxed pace of life compared to mainland Spain, and visitors are often struck by the friendliness and laid-back attitude of the locals. Here are a few customs to keep in mind:

- **Siesta**: Many shops and businesses, particularly in smaller towns, close for a **siesta** in the afternoon, usually from around 1:30 pm to 4:00 pm. It's a good time to have a leisurely lunch or take a break before heading out for more sightseeing.
- **Dining Etiquette**: Canarians often eat later than many visitors might be used to, with lunch typically served between 1 pm and 3 pm, and dinner starting as late as 8 or 9 pm. Meals are a leisurely affair, and it's not uncommon to see locals enjoying a long lunch with family or friends.
- **Festivals and Celebrations**: If you're visiting during a local fiesta or religious festival, don't be shy about joining in. Fuerteventura's festivals are joyful, community-centered events where locals and visitors alike are welcome to celebrate with food, music, and dancing.

Money, Banking, and Tipping

Fuerteventura uses the **euro (€)** as its currency, like the rest of Spain. Most businesses, including shops, restaurants, and hotels, accept credit and debit cards, but it's always a good idea to carry some cash, especially when visiting smaller towns, markets, or local restaurants where card payments may not be available.

- **ATMs**:
    ATMs are widely available in tourist areas, major towns, and shopping centers. Most ATMs accept international credit and debit cards (Visa, Mastercard, etc.), but be aware that some banks may charge a small fee for withdrawing cash. It's worth checking with your home bank before your trip to find out about any international withdrawal fees. To avoid ATM fees, try to withdraw larger amounts at once rather than making multiple small withdrawals..

- **Tipping Etiquette**:

    Tipping in Fuerteventura is generally more relaxed than in some other parts of the world, and it's not always expected. However, leaving a tip is appreciated for good service, especially in restaurants, bars, and cafes. Here are some general guidelines for tipping:

    - **Restaurants**: If you receive good service, it's customary to leave a tip of around **5-10%** of the total bill. If you're just having a coffee or a small snack, rounding up the bill is usually sufficient.
    - **Bars and Cafes**: Tipping is not expected for drinks, but rounding up to the nearest euro or leaving some small change is always appreciated.

- **Taxis**: It's common to round up the fare to the nearest euro when taking a taxi, but tipping is not obligatory.
- **Hotels**: If you receive help with your luggage or special services, leaving a small tip of €1 to €2 for hotel staff is considered polite.

Emergency Contacts and Services

While Fuerteventura is generally a very safe destination, it's important to know what to do in case of an emergency. The island has a well-established network of emergency services, and help is never far away should you need it.

- **Emergency Numbers**:

  The general emergency number in Spain is **112**, which can be dialed for any type of emergency, including medical, fire, and police. Operators can assist you in multiple languages, including English.

- **Police**:
  Fuerteventura has two main types of police forces: the **Policía Local** (local police) and the **Guardia Civil**. The Policía Local handle minor incidents and traffic issues, while the Guardia Civil are responsible for national security and more serious matters. In case of theft, lost items, or other issues, you can report incidents to the nearest police station.
  - Policía Local: **092**
  - Guardia Civil: **062**

- **Medical Emergencies**:

  If you require immediate medical assistance, call **112** or go to the nearest hospital or medical center. For non-urgent medical needs, visit a local **Centro de Salud**, which can provide treatment and advice.

- **Fire Department**:

  In case of a fire emergency, call **080** for the fire department. Fuerteventura's fire services are well-equipped to handle emergencies, but be aware that wildfires can occur during the hotter months, particularly in rural areas. Follow local advice on fire safety, and avoid lighting open fires or barbecues in dry, windy conditions.

- **Lost and Stolen Items**:

  In the unfortunate event that your belongings are lost or stolen, report the incident to the nearest police station as soon as possible. If your passport or other important documents are lost or stolen, you'll need to contact your country's embassy or consulate to arrange for a replacement. It's always a good idea to carry photocopies of important documents, such as your passport and insurance information, in case of an emergency.

Conclusion

Being prepared with practical information can make your trip to Fuerteventura stress-free and enjoyable. By keeping health and safety tips in mind, understanding local customs and language, being informed about money and tipping, and knowing who to call in case of an emergency, you'll be well-equipped to make the most of your time on this beautiful island. Whether you're hiking, sunbathing, exploring villages, or enjoying a festival, Fuerteventura's welcoming atmosphere and easy-going pace will make your visit unforgettable.

• *David O. Terry* •

Day Trips and Excursions in Fuerteventura

While Fuerteventura is a destination that offers plenty to explore within its own stunning landscapes, it's also an ideal base for day trips and excursions that allow you to discover even more of what the Canary Islands have to offer. Whether you're looking to hop over to a neighboring island, take part in guided tours that dive deeper into Fuerteventura's natural beauty and history, or embark on scenic road trips that reveal hidden corners of the island, there's no shortage of exciting adventures to be had.

In this chapter, we'll explore the best day trips and excursions from Fuerteventura, including island-hopping opportunities, guided tours for those who want to learn more about the local culture and environment, and road trips that showcase the island's most scenic drives. Whether you're seeking a day of relaxation or action-packed adventure, these experiences will enrich your visit to Fuerteventura.

Island Hopping: Exploring the Canary Islands

One of the great advantages of visiting Fuerteventura is its proximity to several other Canary Islands, making island-hopping an exciting and accessible way to expand your adventure. Whether you're in the mood for a quick trip to the nearby island of Lobos, or you're interested in exploring the volcanic landscapes of Lanzarote, there are plenty of opportunities for day trips that will add even more variety to your vacation.

- **Isla de Lobos**

    Just a short ferry ride from **Corralejo**, **Isla de Lobos** is one of the easiest and most rewarding day trips from Fuerteventura. This small, uninhabited island is a protected natural reserve and offers a peaceful escape from the hustle and bustle of the mainland. The ferry to Lobos takes just 15 minutes, making it a perfect option for a half-day or full-day excursion.

    Once on Lobos, you can explore the island's beautiful hiking trails, which lead you through volcanic landscapes, pristine beaches, and tranquil lagoons. The most popular hike takes you to the summit of **Montaña La Caldera**, the island's volcanic cone, where you'll be rewarded with panoramic views of Fuerteventura, Lanzarote, and the Atlantic Ocean. For those who prefer to relax, the calm waters of **Playa de la Concha** are perfect for swimming and sunbathing.

    Be sure to pack water, snacks, and sun protection, as there are limited facilities on the island. If you're looking for a peaceful day in nature, Isla de Lobos is a must-visit.

- **Lanzarote**

    Another popular island-hopping destination is **Lanzarote**, located just 30 minutes by ferry from Corralejo. Lanzarote is famous for its dramatic volcanic landscapes, and a day trip here offers the chance to experience its unique natural beauty and fascinating cultural attractions. The ferry between Fuerteventura and Lanzarote runs several times a day, making it easy to plan a day of exploration.

One of the main highlights of a day trip to Lanzarote is **Timanfaya National Park**, where you can see the otherworldly volcanic terrain created by eruptions in the 18th century. The park's surreal landscapes, with their black lava fields and red volcanic cones, are unlike anything else in the Canary Islands. You can explore the park on guided bus tours, or even take a camel ride through the volcanic terrain.

After visiting Timanfaya, you can head to **Jameos del Agua**, a unique cultural and geological site designed by the famous Canarian artist **César Manrique**. This underground cave system, formed by volcanic activity, has been transformed into a stunning space that includes a concert hall, swimming pool, and restaurant.

For a more laid-back experience, you can visit the charming town of **Teguise** or relax on one of Lanzarote's beautiful beaches, such as **Playa Blanca**. Whether you're interested in nature, culture, or simply soaking up the island's atmosphere, Lanzarote offers a fantastic day trip from Fuerteventura.

- **Gran Canaria**

For those looking for a more ambitious island-hopping adventure, **Gran Canaria** is just a short flight or a longer ferry ride away. Although it's a larger island with more to see, it's possible to visit some of its highlights on a day trip if you're up for an early start.

Gran Canaria offers a diverse range of landscapes, from the golden sand dunes of **Maspalomas** to the lush green mountains of the island's interior. A popular excursion is a visit to the historic city of **Las Palmas**, where you can explore the **Vegueta** district with its colonial architecture, visit the **Casa de Colón** (Christopher Columbus House), or relax on the beautiful **Las Canteras Beach**.

For nature lovers, a trip to the **Roque Nublo** area provides stunning views of Gran Canaria's rugged mountains and valleys. Whether you choose to explore the city or the island's natural beauty, Gran Canaria is a fantastic option for those looking to explore more of the Canary Islands.

Guided Tours and Activities

If you prefer to leave the planning to the experts or want to learn more about Fuerteventura's history, culture, and natural environment, guided tours and excursions are an excellent way to dive deeper into the island's treasures. From volcano tours to wildlife watching and cultural experiences, there's a guided activity for every interest.

- **Volcano and Lava Field Tours**

Fuerteventura's volcanic origins have shaped its dramatic landscape, and there are several guided tours that focus on exploring the island's volcanic terrain. One popular excursion is a **volcano and lava field tour**, which takes you to the heart of Fuerteventura's ancient volcanic regions. Local guides will explain the geological history of the island, pointing out unique features like volcanic craters, lava tubes, and ancient basalt flows.

These tours often include visits to sites like **Calderón Hondo**, one of the best-preserved volcanic craters on the island, or the **Malpaís de la Arena**, a vast lava field where you can walk among solidified lava flows. The surreal beauty of these volcanic landscapes is truly impressive, and a guided tour can offer fascinating insights that you might miss if exploring on your own.

- **Dolphin and Whale Watching Excursions**

The waters around Fuerteventura are home to a variety of marine life, including dolphins and whales, making a **dolphin and whale watching tour** a magical experience. Several boat operators in **Corralejo**, **Morro Jable**, and **Caleta de Fuste** offer excursions that take you out to sea to observe these incredible creatures in their natural habitat.

The tours typically last two to three hours and provide the chance to see dolphins playing in the waves and, if you're lucky, spot larger marine animals such as pilot whales or even the occasional sperm whale. Many operators also combine the tour with a stop for snorkeling or swimming, so you can enjoy the clear waters and underwater life of Fuerteventura.

- **Cultural and Historical Tours**

For those interested in learning more about the island's rich history and cultural heritage, guided **cultural and historical tours** offer a deep dive into Fuerteventura's past. These tours often include visits to historic towns like **Betancuria**, the island's first capital, where you can explore ancient churches, museums, and charming streets lined with whitewashed buildings.

Other tours may focus on the island's agricultural traditions, with visits to local farms where you can see how **Queso Majorero** (Fuerteventura's famous goat cheese) is made and taste it fresh from the source. You'll also learn about the island's aloe vera industry, with opportunities to visit aloe farms and try locally produced skincare products.

- **Hiking and Nature Walks**

Fuerteventura's diverse landscapes make it an ideal destination for hiking, and guided nature walks are a great way to explore the island's stunning scenery. Local guides can take you on hikes through Fuerteventura's **Rural Parks**, volcanic areas, and scenic coastal paths, pointing out native flora and fauna along the way.

Popular guided hikes include routes through **Betancuria Rural Park**, where you'll find lush valleys, dramatic rock formations, and traditional farming villages, as well as hikes to the top of **Pico de la Zarza**, the island's highest peak. Whether you're an experienced hiker or a casual walker, there are guided hiking tours for all levels.

Road Trips and Scenic Drives

One of the best ways to explore Fuerteventura is by car, allowing you to take in the island's diverse landscapes at your own pace. With its quiet roads and stunning scenery, Fuerteventura is a perfect destination for road trips and scenic drives. Here are some of the island's most beautiful routes that you can enjoy as part of a day trip.

- **Betancuria to Pájara Scenic Drive**

    The drive from **Betancuria** to **Pájara** is one of the most scenic routes on the island, taking you through Fuerteventura's rugged interior, past volcanic peaks, deep valleys, and ancient villages. The road winds through the **Betancuria Rural Park**, offering incredible views of the surrounding landscapes.

Along the way, you can stop at the **Mirador de Morro Velosa**, a viewpoint designed by Canarian artist **César Manrique**, where you'll be treated to panoramic views of the island's interior. Further along, the village of Pájara offers a quiet, charming place to explore, with its historic **Iglesia de Nuestra Señora de Regla**, known for its intricate Aztec-inspired carvings.

This drive is ideal for those who want to escape the coastal resorts and discover the island's more traditional side, with plenty of opportunities for photography and scenic stops along the way.

- **Corralejo to El Cotillo Coastal Drive**

For a more relaxed and coastal road trip, the drive from **Corralejo** to **El Cotillo** takes you along Fuerteventura's northern coast, offering stunning views of the Atlantic Ocean, volcanic landscapes, and pristine beaches. The route is relatively short, but there are plenty of spots to stop along the way, making it a perfect half-day or full-day excursion.

One of the highlights of this drive is the opportunity to visit the **Corralejo Natural Park**, where you can explore the famous sand dunes and enjoy the beautiful beaches that line the coast. As you continue westward, you'll pass through the quiet village of **Lajares**, known for its artisan shops and laid-back vibe, before arriving in **El Cotillo**.

El Cotillo is home to some of the most beautiful beaches on the island, including the **El Cotillo Lagoons** and **Playa de La Concha**, where you can relax, swim, or take a walk along the coastline. The village also has several great seafood restaurants, making it a perfect spot for lunch or dinner before heading back to Corralejo.

- **Jandía Peninsula and Cofete Beach**

For a more adventurous road trip, head to the **Jandía Peninsula** in the south of Fuerteventura, where you'll find some of the island's wildest and most remote landscapes. The drive to **Cofete Beach** is particularly memorable, as it takes you along a dirt road through the rugged mountains of the peninsula, offering jaw-dropping views at every turn.

While the road to Cofete can be rough, the reward is a stunning, untouched beach that stretches for miles, backed by the dramatic cliffs of the **Jandía Mountains**. This wild, windswept beach is perfect for a peaceful walk or simply taking in the raw beauty of Fuerteventura's untamed coast.

On the way back, you can stop at **Punta de Jandía**, the southernmost point of the island, where you'll find a lighthouse and incredible views of the Atlantic Ocean. This road trip is ideal for those looking for a more off-the-beaten-path adventure and a chance to see a different side of Fuerteventura.

Conclusion

Whether you're interested in island-hopping to discover the unique landscapes of Lanzarote and Lobos, exploring Fuerteventura's volcanic terrain on a guided tour, or taking a scenic drive through the island's most beautiful routes, there's no shortage of day trips and excursions to enrich your experience. With its diverse landscapes, fascinating culture, and proximity to other Canary Islands, Fuerteventura offers endless opportunities for adventure and discovery. No matter which excursions you choose, you'll come away with unforgettable memories and a deeper connection to this stunning island.

Sustainability and Responsible Travel in Fuerteventura

Traveling responsibly and sustainably is more important than ever, especially when visiting fragile ecosystems like those found in Fuerteventura. As a UNESCO Biosphere Reserve, the island's unique landscapes, from its volcanic mountains and sand dunes to its coastal lagoons and rich marine life, are sensitive to the impacts of tourism. By making eco-friendly choices, supporting local communities, and being mindful of conservation efforts, travelers can help ensure that Fuerteventura's natural beauty and cultural heritage are preserved for future generations to enjoy.

In this chapter, we'll explore how you can travel responsibly during your visit to Fuerteventura. We'll offer eco-friendly travel tips, highlight ways to support local communities, and provide insight into the island's conservation and wildlife protection efforts. Whether you're conscious of reducing your carbon footprint, eager to engage with local businesses, or passionate about protecting the environment, these practical steps will help make your trip more sustainable and rewarding.

Eco-Friendly Travel Tips

Sustainable travel begins with small, thoughtful choices that minimize your impact on the environment. Fuerteventura's delicate ecosystems, both on land and in the ocean, can benefit greatly from travelers who prioritize eco-conscious behavior.

Here are some tips to help you reduce your environmental footprint while exploring the island.

- **Choose Eco-Friendly Accommodations**:

    When selecting a place to stay, consider opting for eco-friendly accommodations that prioritize sustainability. Many hotels and guesthouses in Fuerteventura have adopted green practices such as using renewable energy, conserving water, reducing waste, and sourcing local products. Some accommodations, such as eco-lodges and agrotourism properties, are specifically designed to minimize their environmental impact.

    Look for places that have been certified by environmental organizations or that actively promote sustainability on their websites. By choosing accommodations that invest in green initiatives, you're supporting businesses that are committed to protecting the environment.

- **Reduce Plastic Waste**:

    Like many tourist destinations, Fuerteventura struggles with plastic pollution, particularly on its beaches and in the ocean. One of the easiest ways to reduce your impact is to minimize your use of single-use plastics during your trip. Bring a reusable water bottle with you (tap water is safe to drink in Fuerteventura), carry reusable shopping bags, and avoid using plastic straws, cutlery, and cups.

Many shops and cafes on the island are already working to reduce plastic waste, offering eco-friendly alternatives like paper straws or biodegradable takeaway containers. Supporting these businesses and bringing your own reusable items can make a big difference in reducing waste.

- **Use Sustainable Transportation**:

While renting a car is often the most convenient way to explore Fuerteventura, you can reduce your carbon footprint by choosing more sustainable transportation options when possible. Consider renting a hybrid or electric vehicle if available, or use public transportation, which is a reliable and affordable way to get around the island.

If you're staying in a town or resort area, walking or cycling is an eco-friendly way to explore your surroundings, and many hotels offer bike rentals. Fuerteventura's flat terrain and scenic coastal paths make it a perfect destination for cycling, whether you're exploring the countryside or riding along the beachfront.

- **Conserve Water and Energy**:

Water is a precious resource in Fuerteventura, where the climate is dry and rainfall is limited. You can help conserve water by taking shorter showers, reusing towels, and turning off the tap when brushing your teeth or washing dishes. Many hotels also offer the option to decline daily linen changes, which reduces water and energy use.

Similarly, conserve energy by turning off lights, air conditioning, and electronics when you're not in your room. Fuerteventura's sunny climate means that solar energy is increasingly used on the island, but it's still important to minimize unnecessary energy consumption.

- **Respect Local Wildlife and Nature**:

Fuerteventura's natural environment is home to a wide variety of wildlife, including birds, reptiles, and marine life. When exploring the island's beaches, parks, and nature reserves, be mindful of your surroundings and avoid disturbing local wildlife. Stick to designated paths when hiking or visiting protected areas, and never take souvenirs like shells, rocks, or plants from natural sites.

If you're snorkeling or diving, be careful not to touch or damage coral reefs or disturb marine creatures. Avoid feeding wild animals, and always dispose of trash properly to prevent it from harming wildlife.

Supporting Local Communities

Sustainable travel isn't just about protecting the environment—it's also about supporting the local communities that call Fuerteventura home. By choosing to spend your money at locally owned businesses, engaging with local culture, and being mindful of your impact on the community, you can make a positive contribution to Fuerteventura's economy and cultural heritage.

- **Shop Local and Buy Handmade**:

    One of the best ways to support local communities is by shopping at markets, artisan shops, and locally owned stores. Fuerteventura is home to many talented artisans who produce handmade goods, from pottery and textiles to jewelry and leather products. When you buy these items, you're directly supporting local craftspeople and helping to preserve traditional skills.

    Visiting local markets is also a great way to buy fresh produce, cheese, and other food products that are grown or made on the island. By purchasing locally produced goods, you're supporting Fuerteventura's farmers and food producers, while also reducing the environmental impact of imported products.

- **Dine at Local Restaurants**:

    Fuerteventura's food scene offers a wide range of dining options, from beachside cafes to fine dining restaurants. When choosing where to eat, consider dining at locally owned restaurants that source ingredients from the island. Not only will you enjoy fresh, authentic Canarian cuisine, but you'll also be supporting local farmers, fishermen, and chefs who prioritize sustainability.

Restaurants that serve traditional dishes made with local ingredients, such as **papas arrugadas, gofio**, and **Queso Majorero**, offer a true taste of Fuerteventura while helping to sustain the island's agricultural traditions. Additionally, look for eateries that avoid single-use plastics and prioritize environmentally friendly practices.

- **Participate in Cultural Experiences**:

Engaging with Fuerteventura's cultural heritage through local experiences is a great way to support the island's communities. Whether you're attending a traditional festival, taking a cooking class, or visiting a family-run goat farm, participating in these activities allows you to connect with local people and learn about their way of life.

Many villages and rural areas offer **agrotourism** experiences, where you can visit working farms, see how traditional cheese is made, or learn about the cultivation of aloe vera. By choosing to participate in these types of activities, you're contributing directly to the local economy and helping to preserve the island's cultural heritage.

- **Choose Responsible Tour Operators**:

If you're booking tours or activities, look for responsible tour operators that prioritize sustainability and ethical practices. Many operators on the island are committed to minimizing their environmental impact, supporting local communities, and educating visitors about conservation.

For example, wildlife tours that focus on dolphin and whale watching should follow responsible guidelines that prioritize the well-being of marine animals. Look for operators that respect wildlife, avoid overcrowding, and educate guests about the importance of protecting marine ecosystems.

Conservation and Wildlife Protection

Fuerteventura is home to a rich variety of wildlife and natural habitats, many of which are protected by conservation efforts aimed at preserving the island's biodiversity. From marine reserves and bird sanctuaries to efforts to protect endangered species, there are many ongoing initiatives to safeguard Fuerteventura's natural treasures. As a responsible traveler, you can contribute to these efforts by supporting conservation programs and being mindful of your impact on the environment.

- **Marine Conservation**:

    The waters around Fuerteventura are part of a designated **Marine Reserve**, and protecting the island's marine life is a key focus of local conservation efforts. The marine ecosystems are home to a wide range of species, including dolphins, whales, sea turtles, and a variety of fish. To protect these delicate ecosystems, it's important to follow responsible snorkeling, diving, and boating practices.

When snorkeling or diving, avoid touching or standing on coral reefs, as this can cause damage. Always dispose of trash properly, as plastic waste can harm marine life. If you're interested in contributing to marine conservation, some local organizations offer opportunities to participate in beach cleanups or educational programs about marine protection.

- **Birdwatching and Habitat Protection**:

Fuerteventura is a haven for birdwatchers, with several important bird habitats located on the island. The **Salinas del Carmen** and **Barranco de la Torre** are two key sites for migratory and resident bird species, including the endangered **Canary Islands stonechat** and various wading birds. Visitors can enjoy birdwatching in these areas while being respectful of the birds' habitats.

Many of Fuerteventura's bird species are vulnerable to habitat loss due to human activity, so it's important to follow local guidelines when visiting bird sanctuaries or nature reserves. Stick to designated trails, avoid making loud noises, and never disturb nesting birds or their habitats.

- **Endangered Species Protection**:

Fuerteventura is home to several endangered species, including the **Canarian Egyptian vulture** and the **loggerhead sea turtle**. Conservation programs are in place to protect these species, and as a responsible traveler, you can contribute to their preservation by being mindful of your impact on their habitats.

For example, if you're visiting Fuerteventura's beaches during sea turtle nesting season, it's important to follow guidelines to avoid disturbing nesting sites. Local conservation groups often organize efforts to monitor turtle nests and protect hatchlings, and you can support these programs by volunteering or donating to conservation initiatives.

- **Leave No Trace**:

  A simple but powerful way to support Fuerteventura's conservation efforts is by following the **Leave No Trace** principle. This means being mindful of your impact on the environment and taking care to leave natural spaces as you found them. Whether you're hiking, camping, or visiting the beach, always take your trash with you, avoid damaging plants or wildlife, and stick to marked trails to prevent erosion.

  Leaving no trace helps protect Fuerteventura's fragile ecosystems and ensures that future visitors can enjoy the island's natural beauty without causing harm.

Conclusion

Traveling sustainably and responsibly in Fuerteventura is not only about minimizing your environmental impact but also about making thoughtful choices that support the local community and contribute to the preservation of the island's unique ecosystems. By choosing eco-friendly accommodations, supporting local businesses, respecting wildlife, and participating in conservation efforts, you can play a role in ensuring that Fuerteventura remains a beautiful and vibrant destination for generations to come. Whether you're enjoying the island's natural wonders or immersing yourself in its rich cultural heritage, responsible travel will make your experience more meaningful and rewarding.

Conclusion

As your journey through Fuerteventura comes to an end, it's time to reflect on the island's incredible diversity and the unforgettable experiences it offers. Whether you've spent your days basking in the sun on pristine beaches, exploring volcanic landscapes, immersing yourself in local culture, or savoring the flavors of Canarian cuisine, Fuerteventura leaves a lasting impression on all who visit. With its laid-back vibe, stunning scenery, and welcoming locals, this island is a destination where you can truly disconnect, recharge, and create memories that will stay with you long after your departure.

In this final chapter, we'll wrap things up with some practical travel tips, offer suggested itineraries to help you make the most of your time on the island, and give you a warm farewell from Fuerteventura. Whether you're planning a quick weekend getaway or a longer stay, we hope this guide has inspired you to experience the very best of Fuerteventura.

Final Travel Tips and Recommendations

Before you head off on your Fuerteventura adventure, here are some final travel tips and recommendations to ensure your trip goes smoothly.

- **Plan Ahead but Stay Flexible**:

    Fuerteventura is a laid-back destination where the pace of life is slower, so while it's helpful to plan your trip in advance, be open to flexibility. Allow time for spontaneous beach days, leisurely lunches, and unplanned detours to explore hidden corners of the island. You'll often discover that some of the best experiences come from taking things slow and going with the flow.

- **Pack for the Weather**:

Fuerteventura enjoys warm temperatures year-round, but the island's coastal winds can sometimes make it feel cooler, especially in the evenings. Be sure to pack a light jacket or sweater, even if you're visiting in the summer. Sunscreen, a hat, and sunglasses are essential for protecting yourself from the strong sun, and if you're planning on hiking, sturdy shoes and a reusable water bottle are must-haves.

- **Rent a Car for Ultimate Freedom**:

While public transportation is available on the island, renting a car gives you the freedom to explore Fuerteventura at your own pace and visit more remote locations. The island's roads are generally well-maintained and easy to navigate, making road trips a great way to experience the island's varied landscapes. Just remember to fill up on gas when leaving major towns, as petrol stations can be sparse in rural areas.

- **Respect the Local Environment and Culture**:

Fuerteventura's landscapes and wildlife are fragile, so it's important to respect the natural environment by sticking to marked trails, cleaning up after yourself, and following conservation guidelines. When visiting local towns and villages, take the time to learn about and appreciate the island's cultural traditions. A simple greeting in Spanish or an effort to engage with the local way of life will go a long way in making your experience more enriching and enjoyable.

- **Timing Your Trip**:

Fuerteventura is a year-round destination, but the best time to visit depends on your interests. For beach lovers and sunseekers, the warm months of **April to October** are ideal, while **November to March** is perfect for those who want to enjoy outdoor activities like hiking without the intense heat. If you're a surfer or windsurfer, Fuerteventura's winds are strongest in the summer, making it a prime time for water sports.

- **Stay Connected, But Disconnect**:

While it's easy to stay connected on the island thanks to reliable Wi-Fi in most hotels and cafes, Fuerteventura is the perfect place to switch off and enjoy the moment. Take the opportunity to unplug from your devices, tune into nature, and embrace the slower pace of island life.

• **Fuerteventura Travel Guide 2025:** *Uncover the Island's Secrets* •

Suggested Itineraries for Every Traveler

To help you make the most of your trip, here are a few suggested itineraries based on different travel styles, whether you're looking for relaxation, adventure, or cultural exploration.

1. The Ultimate Beach Getaway (3-4 Days)

If you're here to soak up the sun and unwind on some of Fuerteventura's most beautiful beaches, this itinerary is for you.

Day 1:

- Arrive in **Corralejo** and spend the afternoon relaxing at **Grandes Playas**, the wide sandy beaches near the **Corralejo Natural Park**. Watch the sunset over the sand dunes.
- Enjoy dinner at a local seafood restaurant like **La Vaca Azul** in **El Cotillo**, known for its fresh catch of the day.

Day 2:

- Take a ferry to **Isla de Lobos** for a day of hiking, swimming, and relaxing on the secluded beaches of this tiny natural paradise.
- Return to Corralejo for a casual dinner and cocktails at **Waikiki Beach Club**.

Day 3:

- Head south to **Playa de Sotavento** on the **Jandía Peninsula**, one of the island's most famous beaches, known for its calm lagoons and perfect conditions for kitesurfing.
- Spend the night in **Costa Calma** and enjoy a beachfront dinner at **Melia Fuerteventura**.

Day 4:

- Visit the wild and remote **Cofete Beach**, where the rugged beauty and isolation make for an unforgettable final day on the island.

2. Adventure Seeker's Escape (5-6 Days)

For the adventurous traveler, Fuerteventura's diverse landscapes offer plenty of opportunities to explore, hike, and get out on the water.

Day 1:

- Arrive in **Corralejo** and spend the day exploring the **Corralejo Dunes**. Try your hand at sandboarding or take a 4x4 tour through the dunes.
- In the evening, relax at **Rock Island Bar** with live acoustic music.

Day 2:

- Take a guided volcano tour to **Calderón Hondo**, one of the island's best-preserved craters. Hike to the rim for panoramic views.
- In the afternoon, try out a surfing lesson at **Playa del Castillo** in **El Cotillo**.

Day 3:

- Go on a dolphin-watching excursion from **Morro Jable**. Spend the afternoon snorkeling or kayaking along the coast.
- Stay overnight in Morro Jable and enjoy fresh seafood at a local restaurant.

Day 4:

- Hike to the top of **Pico de la Zarza**, Fuerteventura's highest peak, for incredible views over the Jandía Peninsula.
- Relax in the evening at a local restaurant in **Costa Calma**.

Day 5:

- Take a road trip through the rugged **Betancuria Rural Park**. Visit the charming village of **Betancuria** and stop at scenic viewpoints along the way.
- End your adventure with a sunset walk along **Playa de Ajuy** and a visit to the **Ajuy Caves**.

3. Cultural Immersion (4-5 Days)

If you're looking to connect with the local culture, this itinerary focuses on history, artisan crafts, and authentic Fuerteventura experiences.

Day 1:

- Start in **Betancuria**, the island's oldest town. Visit the **Museo Arqueológico** to learn about Fuerteventura's indigenous history and explore the **Iglesia de Santa María**.
- Enjoy a traditional Canarian lunch at **Casa Santa María**.

Day 2:

- Head to **Antigua** to visit the **Museo del Queso Majorero**, where you can learn about the island's famous goat cheese and sample some at the source.
- Explore the local artisan shops in Antigua, known for pottery, textiles, and leather goods.

Day 3:

- Visit the **Centro de Arte Canario** in **La Oliva** to discover contemporary Canarian art. Spend time browsing local galleries and enjoying the town's relaxed vibe.
- Enjoy dinner at **El Horno**, a family-run restaurant known for its traditional dishes.

Day 4:

- Take a guided tour of a local aloe vera farm in **Lajares**, where you can learn about the cultivation of this medicinal plant and purchase eco-friendly skincare products.
- Relax in the evening with a visit to a local **timple** (traditional Canarian guitar) performance.

Day 5:

- End your cultural immersion with a trip to one of Fuerteventura's local markets, such as the **Mercado de los Tradiciones** in **La Oliva**. Pick up handmade crafts, fresh produce, and souvenirs.

Farewell from Fuerteventura

As your time in Fuerteventura draws to a close, you'll leave with more than just memories of stunning beaches and scenic landscapes. You'll have experienced the island's rich culture, tasted its authentic flavors, connected with its welcoming people, and immersed yourself in its natural beauty. Whether you spent your days relaxing on the coast, exploring volcanic trails, or discovering the island's history and traditions, Fuerteventura's unique charm will stay with you long after you leave.

We hope this guide has helped you plan a memorable trip to Fuerteventura and has given you insight into all the island has to offer. As you say goodbye to this magical destination, remember that Fuerteventura's laid-back lifestyle, breathtaking landscapes, and cultural richness will always welcome you back. Safe travels, and we hope to see you again soon!

Printed in Great Britain
by Amazon